Doing the
Math of Mission

Doing the Math of Mission

Fruits, Faithfulness, and Metrics

Gil Rendle

ROWMAN & LITTLEFIELD
Lanham • Boulder • New York • London

Published by Rowman & Littlefield
A wholly owned subsidiary of The Rowman & Littlefield Publishing Group, Inc.
4501 Forbes Boulevard, Suite 200, Lanham, Maryland 20706
www.rowman.com

16 Carlisle Street, London W1D 3BT, United Kingdom

British Library Cataloguing in Publication Information Available

Library of Congress Cataloging-in-Publication Data

Rendle, Gilbert R.
  Doing the math of mission : fruits, faithfulness, and metrics / Gil Rendle.
    pages cm
  Includes bibliographical references.
  ISBN 978-1-56699-754-6 (cloth : alk. paper) — ISBN 978-1-56699-722-5 (pbk. :
alk. paper) — ISBN 978-1-56699-723-2 (electronic) 1. Church management. 2.
Strategic planning. I. Title.
  BV652.R455 2014
  254—dc23   2014014188

∞™ The paper used in this publication meets the minimum requirements
of American National Standard for Information Sciences—Permanence of
Paper for Printed Library Materials, ANSI/NISO Z39.48-1992.

Printed in the United States of America

To the people and the purpose of
the Texas Methodist Foundation

Contents

Introduction

Math and mission may strike some as incompatible at first. Can, in fact, ministry be measured in mathematical proportions? When it comes to a "changed heart," one of the primary experiences of an encounter with Christ, the answer may be that measures of such change are too personal to be easily calculated. When it comes to whether a congregation has been both intentional and fruitful in its mission, the answer is more readily yes—although we have much to learn about the why and the how of such measures. Such learning is a contribution that this book seeks to make.

The mainline church has been hard at work addressing the deep changes required by a changed North American mission field. As I argue in an earlier book, *Journey in the Wilderness*, we are making progress. We have not been idle. The missional church movement, the generational captivity of the mainline church and the current unsustainability of the mainline church have converged to require substantive shifts demanding that congregations, middle judicatories and the denominational church rethink their very purpose. Within my own United Methodist Church, the Council of Bishops has established a "Call to Action" which is an initiative to develop and measure vital congregations. We are experimenting with multiple forms of middle judicatory restructurings. The General Conference, our primary denominational decision-making body, has redefined the work of the district superintendent as a missional strategist in an effort to align strategies of fruitfulness. And there are many examples of congregations refocusing on discipleship and an external missional perspective. This is all evidence of a shift and a growing movement of Wesleyan intent on reconnecting with the culture. Scanning our sister denominations, it is easy to see parallel efforts everywhere across the North American landscape.

However, such change comes with discomfort. At the present moment one of the great discomforts of living into this changed mission field centers on the issue of accountability of leaders and the use of metrics as a tool of accountability. If deep change is difficult, how do we hold ourselves to the task, and how do we measure and guide our progress toward the goal?

"Metrics" refers simply to measurement. Metrics are the tools by which we can ask whether, and how well, intentional efforts toward change are progressing. Increasingly, and appropriately, the Protestant church is learning to ask for accountability of denominational executives, congregational clergy and laity. The use of metrics—middle judicatory dashboards[1] as well as the tracking of congregational efforts—has become an early victim of discomfort and misunderstanding in this search for accountability. I will argue that the use of current dashboard measures of ministry are both necessary and insensitive. They are necessary because a "system gets what it measures." If we don't measure anything, we won't get anything. However, many of the current dashboard measures that we are using are insensitive to cultural and generational shifts in which people no longer join organizations or make decisions, such as baptism, for their children. Our current measures also feel insensitive to clergy who understand their pastoral role to be more "cure of souls" than congregational management. Many clergy feel as if they are being measured by variables, such as church growth, while realizing that they have only limited control over the community demographics of ministry that directly influence that growth.

This book is written from the assumption that our mainline church is only very early in its learning cycle on how to work with metrics and the development of accountability. We are still counting *members* in a time when people who are seeking the church want help in being *disciples*. We are still counting, and giving priority to, a number of congregational variables only because they are easily quantifiable. Given our discomfort and lack of clarity, there is still much for us to learn and much for us to try.

The purpose of this book is to advance the conversation about, and the use of, metrics as a tool of ministry. Our leaders need both more information and more tools to encourage the boldness of actually naming clear outcomes for their ministry and then seeking accountability to move toward those outcomes. Information and tools are also needed to help our leaders shift their understanding of accountability from potentially punitive evaluation to a deeper understanding of accountability as clarity of purpose accompanied by support and encouragement.

A NOTE TO LARGE AND SMALL CONGREGATIONS

One of the rule-of-thumb distinctions given regarding sizes of congregations is that the larger a congregation is, the more it does its work formally (written agendas, reports, proposals, analyses). Conversely, the smaller a congregation, the more it does its work informally (group discussions, leadership conversations, decision making that defaults to past practices). While generally true, the value of this rule of thumb is the reminder that all congregations and middle judicatories do not do their work the same.

What follows in this book is a collection of models, methods and tools of accountability using metrics. Theory is offered to substantiate the models, methods and tools. But when it comes to use—real, on-the-ground application—*appropriateness* is still the required standard.

Large systems may be more formal and data-based in their experiments while smaller systems may choose to be more conversational. The need for appropriate applications, and appropriate leadership in setting outcomes and using metrics, will be further discussed in chapter 5. The starting place, however, is to recognize from the very beginning of this book that systems of all sizes, smallest to largest, need to and are able to be a part of this developing conversation about, and experimentation with, metrics. Appropriateness for leaders means giving attention to both that which addresses the need of the situation and that which also fits the capacity of the congregation or middle judicatory. We are all in this, and there is room for experiments of all sizes and shapes—as appropriate.

ADVANCING THE CONVERSATION

Advancing the conversation is a critical next step. This book is the product of the Leadership Ministry of the Texas Methodist Foundation (TMF; www.tmf-fdn.org) in Austin, Texas, where we are deeply committed to conversation as the currency of change (see www.tmfaplaceatthetable.org as a place where you can join the TMF conversation). From its earlier history as a provider of financial services to individuals, congregations and the United Methodist denomination in Texas, TMF has gone through its own deep change. Intentional and thoughtful discussions and discernments have led TMF to the critical understanding that more than financial resources and services offered by a financial organization are needed by effective people and congregations. Needed also are excellent leadership and a deep culture of purpose if ministry is going to make the difference that God dreams of for our congregations and communities. Through a number of strategies, TMF has been developing a "learning platform" through which leaders can be in conversation with one another to shape their leadership, to develop clear purpose and to develop experiments and strategies for change. To that end, TMF has developed its work of "leadership ministries" to align with its financial services in an effort to help leaders be clear, passionate and strategic in their response to God's call for change in the lives of individuals, communities and the world.

TMF follows a North Star by which it commits itself "to help the Church become more purposeful and more clearly focused on her God-appointed mission through the integration of financial and leadership resources." All such aspirational commitments need to be broken down into discrete and achievable steps. One such step is the development of tools and strategies of metrics. This book is an extension of work that began as a series of five monographs on the use of metrics in the church which were written over a period of fourteen months and made available to leaders through the TMF website. Two national gatherings were held in Austin—one following the release of the third monograph and one following the release of the fifth and final monograph. The purpose of the gatherings was to provide learning conversations where we could teach one another about missional purpose, accountability and metrics.

Because TMF is an edge organization[2] of the United Methodist denomination, the overall tenor of these monographs and this subsequent book will feel Methodist. Nonetheless, while Methodist in character, what is offered here should be easily connected to the efforts and needs of the much wider host of congregations and denominations seeking to be intentional in reflecting God's dream for our present culture.

As in any learning conversation, the hope of this book is that we will lead one another toward new ideas, new actions and greater courage in experiments of faithful change. If conversation is the currency of change, this book is intended as a conversation partner, not as a presentation of conclusions or instructions. To that end this book will serve well if the reader

- takes, uses, adapts and experiments with the ideas and tools to be found here
- approaches the ideas and tools to be found here not as a program or a series of integrated steps to be followed but continually asks herself or himself what might be most helpful to try at any given moment
- shares his or her experience with others to continue the conversation

THE ASTERISK (*)

Throughout this book you will encounter an asterisk (*) as you read. The asterisk indicates that there is a downloadable resource available. Resources and handouts are essential tools of conversations of learning and experimentation because of the way in which they quickly bring focus and common language to the task at hand. The reader will find a list of resources at the end of the book with instructions on how to download them for use in the local setting.

Quite obviously this book is the product of many conversations and collaborations, and so, as writer, I am indebted to many and to all. However, I need to step beyond my more general thankfulness to TMF for providing me a platform for this work and my general thanks to the many leaders who have participated in this conversation with me. In particular I need to thank two colleagues at TMF who have gone beyond their normal responsibilities to shape this project and therefore, this book. In her role as my associate, Teri Fichera has assisted in shaping the metrics project, planned the two national gatherings and provided the editing needed as I write. In her role as vice president of foundation relations, Patti Simmons did the exceptional design and further editing work necessary to make the monographs real tools of conversation. In both cases, I am in their debt for their help, which moved this project to the present book.

ONE

Counting Resources and Measuring Ministry

The conversation about metrics in the church is not a neutral conversation. There is positive energy and distracting discomfort at every point along the way.

AMBIVALENCE AND ANXIETY

Let's begin with our ambivalence. The use of metrics applied to congregations is highly debated with arguments for and against. The arguments supporting metrics often focus on the need to help congregations become more missionally connected with their environment and to become more vital, with an eye to fruitfulness, to intentionally making a difference in people's lives and in their communities. The increased conversation about metrics is an effort to bring a tool to bear on mission and fruitfulness, measuring whether we are or are not making the desired change. To this side of the debate, I can only say, yes.

The arguments against metrics often focus on the unfairness and ineffectiveness of holding leaders accountable for the measure of variables over which they may have only limited, if any, control and the notion that measureable goals, by themselves, do little to motivate or to bring change. The concern is that measures may simply represent institutionalism in a new garb and that it is more just and faithful to trust God to bring fruit from our efforts. To this side of the debate, I can only say, yes.

And then, of course, there are those of my friends who would simply say, "Isn't that just like a consultant to see truth in both sides of an opposing argument." Well, yes, of course. But the fact is there are competing truths here that are very much a part of our faith and our faithfulness. Neither truth holds sway. Neither truth overcomes the other. The presence of these two competing truths is not new for us or for those who went before. In fact, both truths appear within the distance of two chapters of each other in the Gospel of Luke. In the fourteenth chapter, there is a section on the demands of discipleship that call for counting, preparation and intentionality.

> If one of you wanted to build a tower, wouldn't you first sit down and calculate the cost, to determine whether you have enough money to complete it? . . . Or what king would go to war against another king without first sitting down to consider whether his ten thousand soldiers could go up against the twenty thousand coming against him? (Luke 14:28, 14:31)

Clearly the action of leaders is to be directed by measures, and both the builder and the king would reasonably be held accountable for decisions made and actions taken.

However, only two chapters earlier, in the twelfth chapter, there is a warning about worry and the need to trust in God for the future.

> Therefore, I say to you, don't worry about your life, what you will eat, or about your body, what you will wear . . . Consider the ravens: they neither plant nor harvest, they have no silo or barn, yet God feeds them . . . Notice how the lilies grow. They don't wear themselves out with work, and they don't spin cloth. (Luke 12:22–27)

So which is the correct truth? Action or the absence of worry? Accountability or trust? Yes, of course.

If these two different voices can be heard only chapters apart in Luke, I would suggest that they might be found even within the same story in Matthew. In the story that I grew up knowing as the Parable of the Sower (known in the Common English Bible as the Parable of the Soils), "a farmer went out to scatter seed" (Matthew 13:3). The farmer scattered seed all about—some on good soil, some on bad, some by the highway. As a result, some seeds grew and others did not. From this perspective, it is a story of faithfulness. The responsibility of the farmer was to go out and sow—wherever. It was God's task to make seeds grow. Faithfulness is enough because God will make of it what God will. No measures, no goals, no accountability.

Then there is Eugene Peterson's highly regarded interpretation of the same scripture that, in this instance, he calls "A Harvest Story." In this interpretation, the disciples go to Jesus following his story-telling and ask why he tells such stories. Jesus replies,

> You've been given insight into God's kingdom. You know how it works. Not everybody has this gift, this insight; it hasn't been given to them. Whenever someone has a ready heart for this, the insights, the understandings flow freely. But if there is no readiness, any trace of receptivity soon disappears. That's why I tell stories: to create readiness, to nudge people toward receptive insight.[1]

Therefore, this is not a story about faithfulness without measure, but about identifying readiness—which requires measures. It is a story not about when the sower goes out with the seed for the first time; rather, it is about paying attention to results so that when the sower goes out for the second time, previous measures guide a better strategy for sowing seeds. The disciples should learn to recognize readiness, learn to sow the next batch of seeds with those who are ready and those who are willing to become ready. It is about measuring readiness and results, about placing the Word and resources of God in places where they can best grow. More than faithfulness, it is about fruitfulness—about being wise and willingly accountable to make something different happen because of the Word of God.

Intentional planning with measureable outcomes—yes, of course. Faithful ministry with trust that God will make of it what is needed—yes, of course.

When facing competing truths, one is often in a position of needing to choose which of the truths is to be supported *at the moment*. One truth does not outweigh the other, but each in its time will need attention and emphasis. One commentary on Luke's gospel, looking at the same twelfth chapter referenced above, frames the text as the continuation of Jesus's project of transforming his disciples. The commentator wrote, "Still speaking to disciples, Jesus shifts to a new topic. Knowing what time it is and ordering life accordingly."[2]

In our current moment of ambivalence, I simply affirm that it is now time for us to give our attention to the side of the competing truths that requires measures and fruitfulness. We will always be surprised by our God, whose breath will stir life even in the most deadened places. However, we do not have the luxury of not looking for ways to measure and describe vitality and fruitfulness (the richest soils in which to sow our own seeds) so that we can direct our own limited resources to those places most ready to fulfill God's purpose.

If we are ambivalent about metrics, we are also anxious. In one United Methodist Annual Conference, a full gathering of the clergy was invited into a discussion with the bishop about effectiveness in ministry in which the subject of metrics was an integral part. The conference had established dashboard measures that were required to be reported, measures by which congregations would be evaluated. All clergy had been asked to lead conversations in their congregations that focused on goals of ministry. The conversations were to include setting the metrics that congregational leaders would use in order to move the work ahead. The bishop was clear that congregations were accountable for their metrics and that the effectiveness of the clergy would be, in part, tied to the metrics, which quite naturally would have consequences in considerations of current and future appointments.

The anxiety and the energy in the room were palpable during the conversation. However, the responses of the clergy were not all of one piece. There was, of course, a portion of participants who did not care for the conversation but were simply waiting for it to be over so they could return to their congregations, where effectiveness and metrics could be ignored in the future as they had been ignored in the past. There was another portion of participants who were notably upset because their metrics were not positive and they were quite worried about the effect that attention to metrics might have on their futures. There was also a portion of participants who were happy to have the conversation about metrics because their own metrics were positive and because they were committed to counting, already using numbers as a tool of ministry. Curiously, there was a portion of participants, many of them young clergy, who were angry. Their anger came from listening to the bishop explain that measures of fruitfulness and effectiveness in ministry would, in the future, be given attention and used in conversations about the future of ministry for each of the clergy and each congregation. They were angry because they had assumed that such attention to fruitfulness and effectiveness was already an important practice in the conference, and if, in the past, it was not such metrics that determined a pastor's future, then they angrily wanted to know what metrics had been used.

THE NEW WORK IS TO MOVE THIS CONVERSATION AHEAD

We have been in the conversation about metrics for some time now as our congregations and denominations have struggled to live in the changed mission field. As one considers the ambivalence and anxiety in the conversation about metrics, I think it is fair to say we are now at that point where it is unclear whether our conversations represent an effort to clarify or to avoid accountability for the work of ministry. The conversation about metrics is a worthwhile conversation for congregations and denominations to have, but we must steer our efforts toward learning much more about this new task of measurement in the wilderness, rather than simply complaining about the unfairness of being challenged with a changed mission field that makes measurements difficult.

ABOVE ALL, THE NECESSITY OF COUNTING

Let's begin with the simple recognition of the necessity of counting as a responsibility of leadership. One definition of leadership is the ability to draw an accurate and honest picture of the current reality. In most contexts this cannot be done without counting. I have come to increasingly appreciate the story of a regional denomination executive who would begin his work with a personnel committee of a local church by first getting personally acquainted and then asking a series of questions about the congregation, questions such as How many members do you have? What is your average attendance? How many children under the age of five are a part of this congregation? How many youth from the community participate in your ministry to youth? What is the size of your budget and what percentage is supported by current giving? . . . and the questions would go on. The executive tells of meeting with quite a few committees in which the members did not have any answers to these questions and in which people consistently turned to the pastor for answers, only to have the pastor take his or her best guess, without being sure. When it became clear to the pastor and committee members that they did not know the most basic metrics of their own congregation, the executive would then ask how they could expect to fulfill their leadership responsibility of support, evaluation and deployment of their staff if they didn't know about the congregation itself. In order to do even their most basic tasks, leaders need to know the baseline measures of their own institution.

Of course, ministry is about more than describing present reality. Ministry is, more importantly, about some change in a person, a congregation or a community because of the presence of Christ. Such change is the *why* of ministry, and the why does not lend itself so easily to numbers as does the present *what* of the congregation. So, having established the necessity of basic counting of those things countable, we need to go deeper. In his book on leadership from the perspective of the early church fathers, Christopher Beeley states, "Among the many demands that leaders face, the main purpose of pastoral ministry is to guide people toward God in Christ by the power of the Holy Spirit."[3]

In other words, at its heart, ministry is truly not about membership, organizational growth or organizational leadership. Christianity is an alternative narrative to live—a different way of understanding one's world and living in that world that is based not on the power of the culture but on the alternative story from God that makes forgiveness more important than winning, that makes being part of community more meaningful than seeking to control others.

At the heart of ministry is the changed self that comes from an encounter with the presence and story of Christ. Such change is enabled and supported by the ancient model of the purpose of a pastor as one who provides the "cure of souls." The cure of souls is a shepherding of people in which those who need encouragement are encouraged, while those who need to be challenged are challenged. Those who need support are supported, while others who need correction are corrected. The cure of souls and the formation of the individual in faith is an individual process that needs both the support of community and the accountability of covenant relationships. All in all, none of this is easily countable stuff. In other words, the purpose of ministry is much more difficult to measure than is the way we do ministry and the resources we use to do ministry. And yet leaders need always to start from knowing their own institutional baseline counts. This brings us to the issue of vital congregations.

ATTENTION TO VITAL CONGREGATIONS

Formation of people in faith happens in community. Disciples are made in congregations where the body of Christ invites, challenges, models, mentors, supports and provides accountability. While much that happens in the discipling ministry of the local church is not easily countable, the health and vitality of the congregation itself (for which there are more accessible metrics) is an issue of great concern because vital congregations are where formation takes place for many of us. And the health and vitality of the congregation can, to some extent, be measured.

It is at this point that I find the work of my own United Methodist denominational Call to Action focus on vital congregations to be most misunderstood. This United Methodist initiative is not deeply different from the focus on healthy and vital congregations replicated in other denominations. The adaptive question proposed by the United Methodist Call to Action is how the denomination can redirect resources to create more vital congregations. Vital congregations are then defined by measurable metrics. In order to understand progress along this path of denominational renewal, the Call to Action work must be held in proper perspective with the greater denominational mission of making disciples and transforming the world.

If denominational attention to congregations is only about making vital congregations as its end result, as some will argue, then it is appropriately subject to charges of a new institutionalism. In a new institutionalism, the metrics of membership, attendance, baptisms and other countables are merely institutional measures giving anxious attention to needed resources that will sustain the denomination.

However, I will argue that such denominational initiatives, at their best, are seeking to work beyond institutionalism, in a theologically appropriate way, in order to address the larger purpose of making disciples. Vital congregations are not an end result needed by the denomination. Rather, vital congregations are tools needed by the denomination by which mission can be accomplished. Such congregations are not the end but the necessary means to the true end of ministry, which is changing people's lives. If Christians are formed in vital congregations that practice and share the disciplines of Christian formation, and if the mission of the denomination is to make a difference in people's lives, then the denomination needs larger numbers of vital congregations. Currently, using the metrics of the United Methodist Call to Action initiative, only 15 percent of the current thirty-three thousand congregations measure up to being "vital." Like all other denominations, the United Methodist Church must now learn to redirect resources not only toward vital congregations, but also away from congregations that do not evidence either the capacity or eagerness for vitality. (Indeed, this is the application of Jesus's biblical injunction to the disciples to identify readiness as the purpose of the story about the farmer sowing seeds.) To distinguish between vital congregations and non-vital congregations, some agreed-upon descriptors, some better metrics, are needed. What we have found so far in our denominational dashboard measures is only the beginning place for our work on vital congregations. We must learn much more about how to describe and measure vitality of ministry.

The fact remains that it matters whether a congregation is growing or not because growth is a primary indication of whether the congregation is or is not connected to its mission field. It matters how many people are actively engaged in the ministry of the congregation because it is an indication of whether it is a place of emotional and spiritual health that can help people grow in Christ. It matters whether a congregation has "outaged" its surrounding mission field because it is an indication of whether it has the capacity to negotiate generational changes to be able to speak the alternative story of Christ to the new people. It matters.

The bottom line in all of this is that the purpose of a pastor and the purpose of a congregation is to make a difference. Because of the presence of that pastor or that congregation, over time something is to have changed—and how can we have any indication of this change if we do not, in some way, measure?

We now need a conversation that steers away from institutional requirements, defensiveness and avoidance in search of clarity and purpose. The time is ripe for us to mount a new conversation about metrics as a tool of ministry. What is now needed are discerning conversations about purpose and clear outcomes of ministry in vital congregations which are conversations about what God calls us to make different in the mission field where we are placed.

COUNTING AND MEASURING AS SEPARATE TASKS (*1)

Perhaps, when it comes to metrics in the church, it is time for us to distinguish between *counting* and *measuring*. These are both highly related, to be sure, and the distinction I will offer is, to some extent, arbitrary.

Nonetheless, I offer the distinction to make the point that we have been stuck primarily in counting and feeling the limits of our stuck-ness. We now need to move on to measuring. Let's make the distinction this way:

> *Counting is giving attention to numbers.* When counting, the question to be answered is "How many?" Conversations about "How many?" are most frequently conversations about resources. Conversations about resources, in a time of limited resources, are commonly conversations about scarcity—"Do we have enough?" or "How can we get more?"
>
> *Measuring is giving attention to change.* When measuring, the question is not "How many?" but rather "How far?" Conversations about "How far?" are frequently about change that can be measured over time, as in "How far have we come, over the past year, toward our goal?"

There is, of course, room for, and a need for, both counting and measuring. In all complex tasks, multiple tools are needed. However, like all tools, the right tool must be chosen for the job at hand. To that end, it is worth taking a deeper look at the two tools of counting and measuring as separate tools available in our consideration of metrics.

Let me begin with W. Edwards Deming's idea that any system can be understood as constructed of three parts: the input (that which goes into the system); the throughput (that which the system does to, or the way the system uses, the inputs); and the output (or outcome—that difference which the system is trying to make).[4] Figure 1.1 shows a simple diagram of such a system.

At the heart of the church's struggle to be fruitful is a common nonprofit dilemma: nonprofits routinely do not know what difference they are trying to make. In other words, nonprofits (of which churches and conferences are examples) do not know what outcome they are trying to produce.

Deming Simple System

INPUT	THROUGHPUT	OUTPUT / OUTCOME
Resources	**Activities**	The difference or change
(Nouns)	(Verbs)	to be accomplished

Figure 1.1. Simple Systems Model
Source: Patti Simons

In the case of the United Methodist denominational mission, congregations are to "make disciples of Jesus Christ for the transformation of the world." Such a global mission is not only appropriate for the church, it is deeply needed by the world! Where the difficulty seeps in is that a mission for a denomination may be global, but the strategies for the mission must be local. In order to make disciples at the local level, leaders must be able to describe the difference required (the outcome) to move a specific people in a specific location toward discipleship.

In some congregations, the difference needed to move toward discipleship may be as basic as establishing practices of civility within the congregation that will allow leaders to make decisions through other than adversarial ways. In other congregations, discipleship may require a more mature practice of individual accountability for having and behaving with the mind of Christ in each individual's personal life and relationships. The outcome appropriate to each setting of ministry, even to each individual, must be local even though it is part of a global purpose. The outcome appropriate to each setting of ministry is not the same as, but must be related to, the specific needs and gifts of each setting or purpose. The outcome of transforming the world may be as personal as transforming the relationships that an individual has with his or her spouse, children, coworkers and neighbors. For a congregation, transforming the world may be as local as helping a local school increase the percentage of graduates who go on to seek a college education. It may be as global as joining with others to eliminate malaria. However, whatever the outcomes of discipleship and transformation, the local congregation or conference must be able to describe what they believe they are called to produce so they can talk about whether or not they are moving toward their goal.

The word "describe" is used intentionally in reference to outcomes because in nonprofit organizations, outcomes are commonly difficult to reduce to quantifiables. A clear difference is intended and needed, but it is not often easily quantifiable. For example, increased civility within a congregation, as necessary as it is for healthy community, is not easily quantifiable. Not being easily able to quantify a difference does not, however, release one from the responsibility of being accountable to seek making such a difference. Jim Collins has noted that when a nonprofit organization cannot quantify the difference it believes it is called to make, it must be able to richly describe the difference.[5] Without a description there is no way for leaders to have a conversation about whether they are making progress toward their outcome or not. With a stated outcome of increased civility, leaders within the Wesleyan tradition, for example, can at least richly describe Wesley's commitment to holy conferencing and then ask themselves if they have had any unreasonable squabbles at board meetings in the last three months or whether they see themselves moving toward holy conferencing.

Let's now go back to the discussion of the difference between counting and measuring. *Because resources and activities are more easily counted, the temptation of nonprofits, when they are not clear about their outcomes, is to count their inputs and activities.* How many members do we have? How large is our average attendance at worship? How many baptisms; confessions of faith; young people in our youth group; children in Sunday school; volunteers in mission programs? How much is our per capita giving, our budget, our debt? These are all questions of resources and activities, and they are all very countable—they are nouns and verbs. Reggie McNeil has said that the primary dashboards for the mainline church are all about how many, how often and how much.[6] Such dashboard counts are commonly much more related to our inputs and throughputs, our resources and our activities, than they are to our outcomes.

Outcomes are commonly much less "countable" and, as noted in table 1.1, must therefore be richly described. So while the distinction is somewhat arbitrary, for the purpose of moving ahead in our learning about metrics as a tool of fruitfulness, I will argue that counting is what we do with our resources and activities, and measuring is what we need to learn how to do with our outcomes. The distinction between these two tools that I am suggesting is as follows.

Countables are easily quantifiable. We know how many resources we have and how many activities we pursue. We can number and report these even as we argue their importance.

Measurables are more dependent on descriptions of what we feel called to and hope to be able to produce. If we can describe the change that we are called to make, then we can also have discerning conversations about whether we are moving toward that change over time. In chapter 2, I will focus on the critical importance of these outcome descriptions. I will also identify strategies and tools available for measuring outcomes that are not so dependent upon quantifiable numbers.

For the moment, however, consider the following proposals for conversation.

Table 1.1.   Countables—Measurables

INPUT	*THROUGHPUT*	*OUTPUT / OUTCOME*
Resources (Nouns)	Activities (Verbs)	The difference or change to be accomplished
[- - - - - - - - Countables - - - - - - - -]		[- - - - Measurables - - - -]

Counting—Six Propositions to Consider

1. We need to count.
2. While we need to know many things about our churches that can be counted, we are limited when we over-focus on things simply because we know how to count them.
3. Many of the things that we currently count in the church turn out to be insensitive ways to quantify what we think to be important. We are counting membership in an age when people do not join organizations. We are counting attendance at a time when worship is seen as a "program option" by people deeply committed to a search for faith. We are counting baptisms at a time when parents are reluctant to make pro forma decisions that they believe should be made by their child at an age appropriate to understanding.
4. Counting is more often about resources and activities than about outcomes.
5. Counting alone often leads us to conversations about scarcity. When simply counting how many, how often and how much, the conversation naturally goes to what we don't have—our scarcity of resources and activities in comparison to what we wish we had. What is not considered is what we might actually need if we were clear about the local and specific outcome of our ministry.
6. Did you remember number 1? Despite the limits of counting, it actually is necessary to count. One cannot reasonably plan and lead if there is no awareness of resources and activities that can be used for the intended purpose. Leaders need to know their current baseline numbers.

Measuring—Four Propositions to Consider

1. Measuring focuses not on resources and activities but on outcomes— change. Measuring relates not so much to what is but rather what could be. It is more about call, purpose and possibility.
2. Change is a fundamental bottom line of faith, and therefore it is about faith communities. People who have encountered Christ should have behavior that has been changed as opposed to the behavior of those who have not encountered Christ. Christian congregations should be seeking to change the corner of the kingdom of God they have been given (their mission field) because of their faith.
3. The best questions of measure ask both about change and about time: "Over the last six months or a year, how far have we progressed toward the difference that we believe God intends us to make?"
4. Measuring is now at the leading edge of wilderness skills that church leaders need to learn in our journey into a changed mission field.

THE CONVERSATION MUST CONTINUE

While we understand counting, both its necessity and limitations, we still have much to learn about measuring in our churches and conferences. Subsequent chapters will offer observations and ideas for your further consideration and conversation. Measuring requires us to think of our congregations and conferences differently and will require new instruments and techniques. It is all there for us to discover. We have made progress in the wilderness of our changed mission field; but there are now new steps for us to take together.

The first step, however, is to at least not confuse our countables and our measurables. Let us not confuse our resources or activities with our call to make both people and our world different. Let us not confuse our denominational institution with our denominational purpose.

TWO

Getting to Why:
Turning Intentions into Outcomes

Most church boats don't like to be rocked; they prefer to lie at anchor rather than go places in stormy seas. But that's because we Christians view the Church as the object of our love instead of the subject and instrument of God's.

—William Sloane Coffin[1]

Most church organizations I have worked with or been a part of—whether local congregations, middle judicatories or national groups—are much clearer about *what* they do and about *how* they do what they do than they are about *why* they do it. Is there a purpose to what we do? Is it what we do to make some difference in our mission field, in the lives of people, in the communities where we live, in the globe we share? Is there a why behind our anxiety and our activity that would, in fact, provide better direction to what we do and how we do it?

A primary distinction made in the first chapter was a somewhat arbitrary separation of counting and measuring when addressing the issue of metrics. I argue that counting is what we do with our resources and activities, our inputs and throughputs. Counting gives attention to numbers. How many, how often, how much? Measuring, on the other hand, I argue, is what we must learn to do with our outcomes. Measuring gives attention to change. How far have we moved toward our goal? The Deming systems model that I use to make this distinction is in figure 2.1 (*1).

In my experience, counting our resources and activities has had more to do with the church as the object of our love and concern, as expressed in the quote from Bill Coffin above. When counting resources and activities, we are commonly more concerned about whether we have enough and if we are able to protect what we have. We count and then we ask anxious questions of scarcity: How can we get more members? How can we increase stewardship to underwrite the budget? What new programs do we need to start to attract people? How can we protect our buildings, our budget, our endowment?

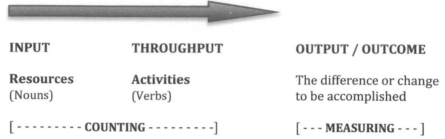

INPUT   **THROUGHPUT**   **OUTPUT / OUTCOME**

Resources   **Activities**   The difference or change
(Nouns)   (Verbs)   to be accomplished

[- - - - - - - - - **COUNTING** - - - - - - - - -]   [- - - **MEASURING** - - -]

Figure 2.1. Simple Systems Model
Source: Patti Simons

I arrived at my first appointment as pastor to a church in Philadelphia soon after they had completed a building project. I was quickly taken aback by the board's unwillingness to consider using our brand-new family-life center for engagement with community people and groups who were not already members of our church, or with other community agencies who shared our purpose of making people's lives better. These leaders in my first church were not mean and uncaring people. Far from it. Their reluctance to use the family-life center simply came down to the issue of the building being brand new, our carrying a substantial mortgage on the building and our lack of available money to deal with someone breaking a window or with increasing our insurance in case someone slipped in the kitchen. These were considered risks that we should take only with our own members where we had an element of control. I could not have said it at the time, but we were too busy loving our church instead of thinking that it had a purpose as an instrument of God's love.

Perhaps such self-love can bleed over into idolatry that even denies a church's purpose, such as the situation I found while consulting with one very large and resource-rich congregation. They spared no expense to build a magnificent children's Christian education center that attached to, and matched perfectly, a flawless, magnificent worship center that sat on the top of a hill. Then they filled the walls of this new children's center with museum-quality art. And finally, they enlisted a core of adult volunteers who came in early on Sunday mornings to monitor the halls to ensure the children did not touch the walls when coming and going. It never occurred to them that they were defeating their own purpose by having a Christian education center where children could not feel comfortable. They could, however, count and re-count for any listener the cost of the building, the value of the art, the expense of upkeep and the size of the endowment used to maintain it.

Conversations about resources/inputs (dollars, time, buildings) and activities/throughputs (programs, groups, projects) easily become worrisome and anxiety-producing conversations about what we have, what we need and how to get more. These are conversations heavily marked by problem solving and either caring for, or fixing, the church we love.

Continuing our distinction, conversations about measuring our outcomes lean more heavily into our purpose—the church not as the object of our love but as the instrument of God's love. This is where conversations turn to discernment and dreaming, and we ask about what we will make different in the lives of the people that we engage, in the communities where we live, in the globe that we share. This is no longer the church as the object of our love but as the instrument of God's love. Conversations are no longer about problem solving, but about possibility hunting.

We know how to count—and we pretty much have in hand the worry and anxiety that accompany counting. It is not with counting but with measuring that we have so much new to learn. Going back to my first appointment again for an example, another of the tussles we had to work through had to do with the baptism of an infant. About year three into my nine-year appointment, I was contacted by an intentionally inactive woman (her name was on our membership roll but she had made it clear that she had been offended by some incident well over ten years ago and would not be back to participate). She had recently become a grandmother, and she called me wanting to know when I would baptize the baby, whose mother I had not met and was similarly a member without connection. I said I would let her know, and I put the request on the agenda of the governing board for a conversation about the expectations we had as a congregation for those who were baptized in our church. I was bothered by my conversation with the woman and thought it would be a good and instructive agenda item for the board's consideration. Somewhat to my surprise, it was a short conversation with the board. My question about under what circumstances would we baptize a baby, despite the clear intent of the family not to have the baby participate in Christian community, was short-circuited by members wanting to proceed without the need for conversation with the mother and grandmother "because you never know what good can come of it years from now."

There it was: "Because you never know what good can come of it years from now." An outcome. We wanted to make a difference in people's lives, so there were multiple and myriad ways in which we engaged people in worship, study, mission and community in that first church I served. But we weren't at all clear about why we wanted to change people and what that changed person might look like if we were successful (faithful). So any hoped-for difference was sufficient—"You never know what good can come years from now from whatever we do now." How does a congregation plan for such diffuse and fuzzy changes? How does a congregation measure its progress toward such an outcome?

The measuring we need to learn how to do must, of necessity, be much more focused and concrete than simply a hoped-for wish. The outcome the church needs is the hope-filled, health-filled, excitement-filled, disturbing differences that God dreams about for our lives and for our communities. Measuring is not worrying about what we don't have. It isn't waiting for what might happen if we just keep doing what we do. The outcomes we need are those deep, and even disturbingly clear, descriptions of what we believe can be different if God gets involved. Again, this is no longer problem solving, it is possibility hunting.

PROBLEMS AND POSSIBILITIES

"The difference between focusing on problem-reinforcing questions and outcome-directed ones is palpable, in terms of optimism, energy, and hopefulness," write Robert Penna and William Phillips in their resource for helping practitioners develop outcomes.[2] Penna and Phillips summarize relevant research, noting that

> highly effective people invest little energy on their existing problem situations. Instead, they focus attention and energy on their desired outcomes or on what they want instead of these problems . . . A key to high performance across all these research contexts has been the ability to develop, articulate and stay focused on a compelling outcome.

To note the difference between problems and possibilities, Penna and Phillips invite the following exercise.

1. Think of a moderately serious problem at work or in your home.
2. Pose and answer these questions:

   Why do you have this problem?
   What caused it?
   Who is to blame for it?
   What obstacles are there to solving it?

3. Now take the same situation and answer these questions:

   What do you want instead of the problem? (Be sure to go beyond merely eliminating the problem.)
   What would it be like if the problem were solved? What would you see, hear and feel?
   Imagine the problem is solved. What has been gained?

I find that the two sets of questions evoke different responses from me, as well as engage different levels of energy. I quite naturally plod into the first set of questions, while the second set engages the energy of new possibilities. It matters how we frame our questions. It matters where we start our discernment and decision making.

SO, WHAT IS AN OUTCOME? A WORKING DEFINITION (*2)

The intention of this book, and the conversations that will accompany it, is that we will teach one another better responses to this question about what an outcome is. For nonprofit organizations, the shaping and use of outcomes is a perennially difficult task. For the moment, I will offer a place-holding definition of an outcome while we work together to get more clarity: *For the church, an outcome is (1) the difference that (2) you believe God has called you to make (3) in this next chapter of your life.* An outcome is

1. *A measurable/describable difference.* The fundamental and obvious proposition of the Christian faith is that because Christ is in our lives, something should be different. We should be different. Our relationships with others should be different. What we give ourselves to should create a difference. We are not here to preserve and protect but to challenge and change.
2. *You believe God has called you to make.* That is, the product of the purpose God has given you—what is to be different—is not about our preferences but about God's purpose. The outcome of a congregation is not about what we can think of to do next but about what God calls us to make different. A faithful outcome of healthy ministry requires more discernment of God's will than decision making about our own future.
3. *In this next chapter of your life.* So it is to be accomplished in a clearly defined, and relatively brief, period of time: an outcome is not for all time but is the necessary next step of development toward the larger dream that God has but which we cannot yet fulfill. Outcomes are time limited. They are about what we need to learn how to do, how to live, next.

DIFFERENCE AND TIME

For us to move ahead, we need to take seriously the connection of time with our outcomes of ministry. Not to do so allows us the easy escape of idealists who are so captured by the ultimate hope that they easily sidestep the reality of proximate requirements. We can so easily dream of and hope for God's peaceable kingdom that we refuse to engage the reality that to get there we must first cage some lions and also encourage some lambs. The temptation is to allow hard work to be displaced by wishful hope.

This is the current dilemma of many of the denominations that I have written of in earlier projects. In the case of United Methodists, we are now a people whose mission is to make disciples of Jesus Christ for the transformation of the world. Like other mainline denominations whose congregations follow a clearly defined membership model, the shift from making members to making disciples is a frame-bending challenge. We want disciples—people changed by their encounter and engagement with Christ. We want a transformed world—a place changed by the differences that disciples bring to relationships, to setting priorities, to redirecting resources, to addressing the needs of others instead of their own preferences.

However, it is easy to get captured by the wishfulness of such a big dream and miss the hard work of the first steps. We are now a people who want to make disciples, but we have congregations where disciple-ship is not being practiced. We expect God's peaceful kingdom to be birthed from congregations that are contentious about their own deci-sions. We want to include others in denominational purpose as long as they worship in our preferred ways, serve on committees and remain loyal to our institution. If we want to make disciples of Jesus Christ for the transformation of the world, there is a lot of hard work to do. It is this proximate hard work of the "next steps" of our mission that is the appropriate subject of measurable/describable outcomes. What is the specific difference that God asks you or me (not some generalized "we" or "they") to address in this next chapter of our lives and work? If we get this right and work at it, then we can ask again in three to five years the same question about what God calls us to do next, moving step by step from institutionally making members to missionally mak-ing disciples.

A short story I have been using in my consulting with middle judicato-ries, and have written about elsewhere, concerns a mother who sends her young son out on a pitch-black night to be sure the barn door is locked on the family farm. He leaves but comes back inside within seconds. When his mother asks what is wrong, he says he can't do what she asked because the night is too dark and he can't see the barn from the house. So the mother hands him a flashlight and sends him out again, only to have him return a second time in less than a minute. When she asks what's wrong this time, the son says that he still can't find the barn because the flashlight isn't strong enough for him to see that far. The mother sends him out a third time, saying he doesn't need to see the barn. "Just walk to the end of the light," she instructs her son.

When one walks to the end of the light, the next portion of the path is revealed. All the young boy needs to get started is a conviction that the barn lies out there in a particular direction rather than some other direction. Then as he goes, the path will be revealed sufficiently to allow him to proceed and make corrections in direction until the barn is found. This is where we are as a church at this moment. We are called to make disciples. We are called to change the world. But to do so, we must take some proximate steps that will make some immediate differences so that we follow a path that will lead us to our ultimate mission.

These necessary proximate steps are what our attention to vital congregations is all about. Picking up the conversation begun in the first chapter, we do not need more vital congregations for the sake of having better congregations that can reverse our membership decline, offer better programs or pay better clergy salaries. To focus on vital congregations in such a short-sighted way would simply be another step toward empty institutionalism—a form of loving our church instead of using it. But we do need vital congregations because vital congregations are where people's lives are changed. Vital congregations are that next step—that proximate outcome—that we, as denominations, must pursue. In order to fulfill our mission of making disciples, we need more vital congregations—so vital congregations are the necessary tool that we must learn to construct in order to make the church the instrument of God's love.

The current task toward addressing our ultimate mission is to learn how to turn our disciple-making intentions into measurable/describable outcomes—plausible, doable next steps. In our best examples this is why some of our denominational middle judicatories are restructuring, reprioritizing and redirecting resources and focusing on the mission field within their bounds, instead of simply caring for the congregations, clergy and committees that make up their constituency. In our best examples this is why some of our most vital congregations are prioritizing ministry with specific groups of people and focusing on making just one or two specific but significant changes in their neighborhood within the next five years.

The criteria of time helps us to focus on doable differences. In the next six months, one year, three years . . . what is the specific difference that you or your congregation is called to make? Answering this question, with its constraint on time, is a step toward a faithful and effective outcome.

LEARNING TO TALK ABOUT OUTCOMES INSTEAD OF PROCESS

It may well be that in order to learn how to work with outcomes, we will need to first learn how to ask questions that prompt outcome responses. As noted above, it matters what question one asks because within the question is a clue to the answer. I love the old story of the priest who went to his superior to ask if he could smoke while he prayed, only to be told "No." Another priest went to the same supervising father to ask if he could pray while he smoked, to which the answer was "Yes, of course, my son." It matters how we ask the question.

Again, using the contrast between counting, which gives attention to resources and activities, and measuring, which gives attention to outcomes and differences, there is a way to distinguish the kinds of questions we use as we work. Resources and activities are based on process. The difference we seek is based on outcomes. Consider the distinction offered by Penna and Phillips in their work on outcomes (see table 2.1; *3).[3]

Notice how the questions of process lead to answers of activities and resources. We provide services. We offer group and individual counseling. We provided 500 hours to 125 families. The answers reflect the good work that the organization does. But they offer no real clues to the differences the organization is trying to make beyond the wishfulness to be of help and the hope that it is working. If one is a counselor in such an organization, it would be very possible to become tired after many hours, much effort and significant worry about those needing help without any conviction that one's work is making any measurable difference.

Consider the difference when asking outcome-focused questions (see table 2.2).

It is only when driving deeper into outcome-focused questions that we discover that the difference this organization is going to focus on is parenting skills in abusive families as measured by the use of corporeal

Table 2.1.   Process-Focused Questions and Answers

Process-Focused Interview
Q. What does your organization do?
A. We provide services to low-income residents of our community.
Q. What kinds of services?
A. We provide group and individual family counseling.
Q. How many people do you serve?
A. Last year we provided 500 counseling hours to 125 families.

Table 2.2. Outcome-Focused Questions and Answers

Outcome-Focused Interview

Q. What is your organization hoping to accomplish?

A. We are working to improve the parenting skills of abusive families.

Q. What kind of skills improvements are you working toward?

A. Reductions in use of corporeal punishment and increases in uses of positive reinforcers of good behavior, among others.

Q. For the coming year, what level of results would make the year a success?

A. For the coming year, we are working to improve parenting behavior in 200 families (as measured by the use of corporeal punishment or the use of reinforcement of good behavior).

punishment versus positive reinforcement of good behavior. To focus on parenting skills may not cure all the ills of families in the community, but it is a clear, proximate outcome that, if well addressed, can move the community closer to becoming a healthy environment in which children can be formed.

Consider the table provided by Penna and Phillips in which process and outcome questions are viewed side by side (see table 2.3).

Notice again how process-oriented questions focus in on problems—what problems are you trying to fix, what problems do you have to figure out in order to fix things? Outcome-oriented questions invite possibility. What could be different if you do your work well?

Table 2.3. Comparison of Process- and Outcome-Oriented Questions

Process-Oriented Question	Outcome-Oriented Question
What housing services do you offer?	What community results do you hope to accomplish through your housing services?
What is it that your agency does?	What is your organization striving to achieve?
What service needs does your agency meet?	What changes in conditions or behavior are you attempting to effect in the people you serve?
What services must we offer to prevent our community from further deterioration?	What would be the ideal mix of people and businesses to make our community more desirable?
How can we overcome the learning challenges students bring with them to school?	What skill sets and knowledge must our children possess to be successful?
What public-information strategies do you use?	What changes in attitude are you attempting to effect and with what specific groups?

STEPPING BEYOND FUZZY IDEAS AND FUZZY LANGUAGE

The fact is that one of the primary reasons congregations and denominations (like all other nonprofits) tend to live comfortably with process
questions is that it is hard for us to be clear about what we are actually
trying to make different, and it is equally hard for us to know if we are
making the desired difference since we have only limited control of either
the subject or the environment of our change.

Working in the for-profit world is not automatically easy work. It
is frequently complex and difficult. Leadership can be buffeted by
changing industry standards, shifting economies and paradigm shifts
from local to global markets. Nonetheless, it is easier for leaders in a
for-profit organization to identify clear, measurable, quantifiable outcomes. At their most basic level, both the input and the output of a
for-profit organization are clear and quantifiable. What goes into a for-
profit organization is money. It is a quantifiable input with which the
organization will purchase raw materials; build and maintain facilities;
hire a workforce of producers and managers; and comply with human
resource laws, tax laws and a whole host of requirements, as well as
oversee production, marketing and delivery systems. And while the external market for which the work is to be done is not controllable, there
are multiple measures of production and employment-based accountability that make the internal environment significantly more controllable. The work is complex. But note also that the desired outcome in
a for-profit organization, what is to come out of the system, is equally
clear. The desired outcome is more money coming out than what went
in. Like the input, the output too is quantifiable. Effective for-profit
organizations are rarely fuzzy in their outcomes or their measures,
which makes it easier to determine the resources and activities needed
to produce the desired outcome.

Again, picking up the conversation begun in the first chapter, the critical difference between for-profit and nonprofit organizations, as noted by
Jim Collins, is that nonprofits routinely do not know what they are trying
to produce.[4] Management leader Peter Drucker, in one of his earlier books
that quickly became a standard in the nonprofit world, said that the outcome of all nonprofits is an improved human being.[5] As true as the effort
to "improve human beings" is, it is not an outcome that invites critical
thinking about how to do it. What is the clear and specific improvement
in a human being that a nonprofit organization is trying to make? What
is the clear, proximate outcome needed to move one more step closer to
that improved human being? These are actually very difficult questions
for most nonprofits, obviously including congregations and annual con-

ferences. It isn't until we get clear and specific about the difference we are trying to effect (in the next three to five years—don't forget the importance of providing a time frame) that we can move toward measuring progress toward our outcome.

Specificity brings clarity: We are going to improve the community by reducing corporeal punishment in abusive families and replacing it with skills of positive behavior reinforcement. We are going to make disciples by first behaving like disciples, reducing the number of arguments in our board meetings that define people as winners or losers and replacing those arguments with skills of careful listening and questions of discernment that will lead us to decisions connected to our purpose rather than our competing preferences. We are going to transform the world by increasing the percentage of young people in the school across the street from us who go beyond high school for college or technical training. Moving from fuzzy intentions to clear differences is a significant challenge to the church's ability to fulfill its mission.

The difficulty of getting such clarity about what we in a congregation or an annual conference actually produce is one of the reasons we are so familiar and so comfortable with process conversations rather than outcome conversations. Collins points out that when an organization is unable to measure its outcomes, it frequently measures its inputs and its throughputs—its resources and its activities.[6] As noted in the first chapter, How many? How often? and How much? are the current dashboard measures of the mainline church. These are all measures of resources and activities.

We remain focused on inputs and throughputs because outcomes are so difficult. It is a dilemma we share with other nonprofit organizations. For example, in 2011 a project was mounted to analyze the mission statements of sixty prominent museums that exhibit contemporary art. The inspiration for this project was a question about museum missions: What is the purpose of a museum? One result of the project was to note that there was very little consensus that could be found by analyzing the words museums used in their mission statements. However, many of the words described core functions—"collect," "educate," "exhibit," "preserve." Note that these are essential activities/throughputs. They are verbs, actions, strategies. In similar fashion, the church often describes itself as providing worship, Christian education and missional outreach—also verbs, actions and strategies. Like the statements of museums that collect, educate, exhibit and preserve, our description of a church that provides worship, education and outreach is not a statement of what we are called to accomplish but rather of the activities that we practice in the hope that something is accomplished.

Perhaps the most telling part of the report on the analysis of museum mission statements is the following.

> One pattern that does seem to cut across categories is the vogue for anodyne formulations that set no tangible goals and forestall accountability. Museums all too often strive, engage, foster. Variations on this theme abound: advance, seek, aim, sustain, affirm, focus, honor, consider, invite and so on. To the dismay of foundation and government officials, there is little in this vocabulary to lend itself to measurable outcomes. Lack of specificity, in fact, may be the one trait that mission statements have in common.[7]

"Anodyne formulations." I had to look that one up—"anodyne," meaning "not likely to provoke offense or dissent." In other words, the mission statements of the museums were written so as to not offend or discomfort anyone, including those who wrote the statements. Now assuredly mission statements are not the same thing as clear outcomes, and they are not meant to be. But the hint here is that perhaps our understanding of mission and our work on outcomes in the church may be hampered by our unwillingness to be so clear that it might actually offend or lead to discomfort or disagreement. As long as we remain general, using fuzziness as a guideline, it is not likely to upset what we know and what we do. It is sufficient to attend to our activities "because you never know what good can come of it years from now."

The mission statement in the United Methodist Church, however, clearly insists that we are supposed to be provoking and discomforting. Becoming a disciple of Christ is not being affirmed for who we already are, it is the discomforting confrontation of who we are not yet. The conversation Jesus had with Nicodemus, the rich young ruler, and almost everyone else in the Gospels, was a discomforting event in which people were individually given a question or challenge they needed to wrestle with. Similarly, the world will not be transformed passively with general intents. Transformation is the hard, specific work of seeing that something that is wrong becomes right, something that is dark is brought to the light, something that is not yet is brought into being. Perhaps the most effective outcome is one that "offends" in its clarity. It risks describing very clearly something that is not yet. And certainly part of the risk is that we are not sure how to bring about the change.

Consider a nonprofit example from outside the church. Muhammed Yunus, founder of Grameen Bank, received the Nobel prize for his pioneering work in microlending to the very poor in Bangladesh. Like other lending institutions, Grameen Bank uses obvious process metrics of numbers of borrowers, size of loans, rate of repayment and other profitability indicators. These, however, are just the measures of inputs and throughputs, the resources used and the activities pursued in making loans. The real purpose of Yunus's work is to change the socioeconomic situation of the bank's members and to move people out of poverty. One could simply offer loans and hope that it would help people out of poverty. But Grameen Bank did the hard work to precisely define "out of poverty" by developing its ten indicators.[8]

*The Grameen Bank Ten Indicators (*4)*

A member is considered to have moved out of poverty if his or her family fulfills the following criteria.

1. Family lives in a house worth at least Tk. 25,000 (about $350) or a house with a tin roof, and each member of the family is able to sleep on a bed instead of on the floor.
2. Family members drink pure water out of tube-wells or boiled water or water purified by using alum, arsenic-free purifying tablets or pitcher filters.
3. All children in the family over six years of age are going to school or have finished primary school.
4. Minimum weekly loan installment of the borrower is Tk. 200 (about $2.80) or more.
5. Family uses sanitary latrine.
6. Family members have adequate clothing for everyday use, warm clothing for winter, such as shawls, sweaters, blankets, etc., and mosquito-nets to protect themselves from mosquitoes.
7. Family has sources of additional income, such as a vegetable garden, fruit-bearing trees, etc., so that they are able to fall back on these sources of income when they need additional money.
8. Borrower maintains an average balance of Tk. 5,000 (about $70) in his or her savings account.
9. Family experiences no difficulty in having three square meals a day throughout the year, i.e., no member of the family goes hungry at any time of the year.
10. Family can take care of its health. If any member of the family falls ill, family can afford to take all necessary steps to seek adequate health care.

In addition to defining specific outcomes for each member, the Grameen Bank defines specific outcomes for each bank branch.

1. Borrowers repay 100 percent of their loans.
2. The branch is profitable.
3. Deposits are greater than outstanding loans.

4. All children of each member are in school or have completed at least primary school.
5. All members have crossed over the poverty line.

With such clear definition of outcomes, for both the borrowers and for the branch banks, the risk of "offense" is palpable—either one measures up to the mark or does not. Far from wishful thinking and hoped-for results, the clarity by which being out of poverty is defined gives very clear goals to both the borrower and the bank.

TURNING INTENTIONS INTO OUTCOMES— MOVING FROM THE WHATS AND HOWS TO THE WHYS

The argument of this book is that faithfulness to our purpose requires that we go beyond intentions to the hard work of purposefully making a difference. To do so requires that we change our language and our measures from general to specific and from process to outcomes.

For example, one of the more helpful and influential books in recent years is *Five Practices of Fruitful Congregations* by Bishop Robert Schnase. The book gives sharp focus to the five practices of radical hospitality, passionate worship, intentional faith development, risk-taking mission and service, and extravagant generosity—all of which are acknowledged by the author as "congregational activities"; that is, throughputs. In the introduction Bishop Schnase writes,

> This book is designed to assist congregational leaders in holding a mirror to their own ministries in order to ask the questions "How are we doing in practicing these qualities of ministry in our congregation? In our classes, choirs, small group ministries, mission teams, and leadership circles? How are we practicing these in our personal discipleship? And how might we do better?" The task of repeating, deepening, extending, teaching, and improving these practices would fill church agendas, guide church boards, and shape leadership training.[9]

But this is still conversation about activities—activities of excellence, to be sure, but activities nonetheless.

These are the right conversations for our leaders to have so that our congregations become more vital and move closer to making disciples. Bishop Schnase writes, "People know that the mission of the church is to make disciples of Jesus Christ but they are seeking to understand how to fit this larger mission into their lives and into their church in a practical way." It is this shift to the practical and specific level (the proximate outcomes) that requires clarity of outcomes. It is the search for proximate next steps by which we get clear about what any one of the five practices would look like "on the ground" in our own congregation. For instance, to be radically hospitable, a congregation and its leaders must have both the subject of their hospitality and the difference their hospitality is to make clearly in mind.

In my second pastoral appointment, which was located in the urban center of one of our Pennsylvania cities, our surrounding neighborhood was 40 percent African American, 40 percent Hispanic and 20 percent white Anglo. It was clear that there were churches in place to serve the African American and the white Anglo populations but that there were few Hispanic churches, and none in our section of the city. So the congregation I served set out to establish a new Hispanic congregation, with our own heavily used building as the starting home for this new ministry. We were hospitable—friendly, inviting, welcoming. We even designated our chapel as the Hispanic congregation's worship space. However, at one point the relationship between our Anglo congregation and the new Hispanic church broke down as we argued about the appropriateness of storing snow tires from the Hispanic church's van in the chapel we designated for their use and which was still seen as sacred space to be used in accordance with the standards of the Anglo church. If we (the Anglo congregation) wanted to provide the ministry of the church to make disciples among our Hispanic neighbors, we needed to get much clearer about our own radical hospitality. Sadly, our hospitality remained an intent rather than an outcome. Had we done the necessary hard work of defining clear, measurable/describable outcomes, we would have had a Grameen Bank–like list of descriptors of our hospitality which would surely have included "Our Hispanic guests will have the agency to determine how they will use their own space" as one of the measures to change our intent of hospitality into an outcome of hosting the birth of a new congregation. Without such clarity our hospitality spoke mostly of our missional intent and the kindness of our hearts without making our Hispanic brothers and sisters feel as if they belonged in the space we provided. Tellingly, during our dispute over the use of the chapel space, one of the Hispanic leaders said, "It is good to be invited into our brother's house" (meaning our Anglo church). However, he continued, "we are constantly reminded that it is our brother's house." If our intent was clear to us, our outcome was not.

Recently in my consulting with a large community church, I learned of their new missional goal to provide ministry "to those who have been damaged by the Christian church." This group of leaders did the necessary discernment and hard work to see these people in their community and to discern that they had the capacity to invite these people into a disciple-making relationship with their church despite the experience of these people in other congregations. Their intent was in place.

However, to move past intentions to get to outcomes, this congregation was going to have to define their hospitality well beyond the limits of friendliness in order to develop a strategy of how to identify, invite, welcome and provide safe space in their congregation to these particular people. They would also have to be able to clearly describe what it would look like for a person to have overcome previous "damage." To accomplish their outcome they would need to "build their system backward," an idea that will be explored in the third chapter of this book. For the moment it is enough to say that the clearly understood "audience" of their ministry—those who had been damaged by the church—would need equally clear measures of the difference in the hospitality required to bring these people back into an institution that they would prefer to avoid because of past experience.

The why of a radically hospitable congregation is to make a change in people's lives—something that is best done within the context of Christian community. Until we get the why of our congregations and denominations right, the whats and hows are simply activities. But once we are clear about the why, get focused on the specific who and name the clearly defined outcome that we are called to provide, the whats and the hows will be able to move beyond a simple friendliness that believes that if we are nice to people, "you never know what good can come from it years from now."

CLARITY AS A WAY OF LIVING AND
THRIVING AS A FAITH COMMUNITY

In the years that North American denominations have been experiencing shrinking membership and resources we have learned quite a bit about leadership. Where we once defined leadership in terms of the decisions a leader made on behalf of others, the most recent focus has been on the conversations that leaders invite others into. Conversation is the currency of change. What we invite people to talk about, to think about, to pray about determines the path that we will follow into the future. Leaders have the power of agenda—they have the responsibility of determining what a congregation or denomination will focus on by giving time and attention to a conversation. A primary act of leadership is to be able to develop an agenda for conversations which tells people that it is more important for us to talk about "this" than to talk about "that." The argument of this chapter is that in very many settings it is more important for us to talk about outcomes than to talk about resources and activities.

We are currently in a moment in which there are three essential types of conversations that leaders can invite others into: maintenance conversations, preferential conversations and missional conversations (*5).

Maintenance conversations have a primary focus on preserving who we were and following the rules already set. For example, in my United Methodist tradition there is great value in remembering and preserving our evangelical roots and our "methodical" purpose of spreading scriptural holiness throughout the church and across the nation. However, maintaining too many of the norms, policies, rules and traditions that we have accrued along the way can be stultifying to a people who now need to gather energy and courage to enter into a changed cultural mission field where old ways have become ineffective. Maintenance conversations have their place but easily undermine the very mission that we claim for making disciples.

Preferential conversations focus on satisfying the people who are already in our congregations or focus on attracting the people that we wish were in our congregations. Preferential conversations also have an appropriate place in our work. The Word of God, and the invitation to discipleship, will be heard by people only when we understand the unique preferences by which they will respond to involvement and engagement with others and with the issues of a changed life. In any mission field, the carriers of the Good News have to first learn the language and the ways of the indigenous people. Preferential conversations, however, easily slip into judgments about the right way and wrong way to go about things. When we are focused only on preferences, the way in which something is done easily trumps the importance of doing it. At its most limited, preferential conversations devolve into the search for ways to keep people happy and unchanged instead of being challenged and reshaped by the demands of the Gospel.

Missional conversations focus on purpose and on the possibility of the future. The origin of the word "mission" is mid-sixteenth century, denoting the sending of the Holy Spirit into the world, from the Latin *missio*, meaning "sending," or *mittere*, meaning "to send." To send is to talk about what is not yet, what is possible with the sending of the Holy Spirit. It is here that clarity of purpose and outcomes is most important in order for us to participate with the Holy Spirit to address that which is not, yet, accomplished. Discernment about what God dreams for us, and for which God sends his Spirit, requires a specificity about what is yet to be if we are to be the helping hands to make it so.

We are clear about our maintenance and our preferential conversations. We know quite a bit about our past performance, norms and rules. Fingers continue to be pointed at who did what wrong as well as what cannot be done because it lies outside of our rules. We are quite clear about our preferences and who likes to do what in particular ways. The worship wars of the recent decades have been remarkable examples of preferential battles. What is now needed is conversation about clarity of mission. Who are we now? What has God called us to make different, now? Who is our neighbor, now?[10] In the long struggle to understand our current situation as a denomination and as congregations, our attention is now being increasingly drawn to the need for clarity of outcomes—clear statements of purpose as defined by the specific difference we are called to make. The Hartford Institute for Religion Research released its most recent report on church growth in 2011, in which it offered a number of congregational activities and orientations that either positively or negatively correlated with congregational growth. Tellingly the research report confirmed once again earlier research stating that "one of the stronger correlates of growth was the extent to which a congregation has a clear mission and purpose."[11] Clarity of mission and purpose requires specificity. It needs the identification of the clear and specific difference that is to be made in order to be faithful and fruitful. It needs clear outcomes that are describable. And it needs clear measures that enable us to know whether we are moving in the right direction or not.

It is to this specificity of outcomes and measures that must be unique to each setting of ministry that we will turn our attention in the next chapter. For despite the good work that has been done in efforts of congregational transformation and with the repurposing of our denominational judicatories and agencies, there are no standardized or programmatic answers that we will find to determine what any single congregation or denomination must do. It depends on the difference that each is singularly and uniquely called to make. There is still more for us to consider in this work of getting clear about what we must change in order to get closer to God's dreams for us.

THREE

Phronesis and the Task of Figuring It Out for Ourselves

Cat: Where are you going?
Alice: Which way should I go?
Cat: That depends on where you are going.
Alice: I don't know.
Cat: Then it doesn't matter which way you go.

—Lewis Carroll, *Alice in Wonderland*

Congregations and denominations, like most nonprofit organizations, notoriously don't know where they are going or what difference they are trying to make. Congregations and annual conferences, like all nonprofits, are driven by an ideal. People should be healthy. Abuse should stop. The ecology should be protected. Christians should behave as disciples of Christ. Beyond their stated ideal, it is difficult for nonprofits, including congregations and annual conferences, to get specific about what must change or be accomplished in order for the ideal to come closer to reality. We know what we do (our normal activities), but we have lost our certainty about why we do it (our purpose). Having lost certainty about why we are to act, we have simply acted with certainty—and, in the case of the mainline church, we have pursued what we already know how to do with such certainty that we have lost relevance to a world that has changed around us. As Yogi Berra famously said, "If you don't know where you are going, you'll end up someplace else."

With a clearly defined outcome before us, we can measure our way toward making a difference; and with an outcome shaped by the presence of Christ in our lives and in our communities, we will find ourselves and our congregations both fruitful and relevant. Without a clearly defined outcome that describes what is to be, we are left only counting what is—how much and how many we have, how much and how many we wish we had.

37

THE NECESSITY OF OUTCOMES

Consider the example of a well-established and vital Presbyterian church in the Midwest with a widely known reputation for its adult Christian education program. The program was centered around regular Sunday morning lessons taught by regional and national experts who could, at times, include former presidents of the United States, Nobel Prize–winning scientists, or acclaimed and prize-winning poets. The church leaders were very proud of their program and the resources they spent on its excellence and reputation.

In the midst of very careful strategic planning in this congregation, some data was brought to the attention of the adult education staff and leaders by the planning team. Over the past five years, two very clear trends had developed in the participation level of people in this church. The first trend showed that participation in the highly acclaimed adult education program was clearly shrinking. The second trend was that the number of children, nursery level through sixth grade, was growing rapidly. The planning team was raising a question informed by the data: there were clearly more and more children in the Christian education program who were being brought to the church by their parents, but there was no parallel growth in the adult program to reflect the participation of those parents. What was going on?

The planning team convened two small groups of parents whose children participated in the Sunday school program but who, themselves, did not participate in the adult education offerings. Yes, the parents knew about the exceptional adult education opportunities at the church. And, yes, after dropping off their children for Sunday school, many of the parents went off to Starbucks as couples, sometimes as small groups, for conversation. When asked why by the planning team, the basic message was Yes, the parents knew who was speaking at the adult gathering, but after a pressured and hectic week of attending to work, family and everyone else's needs, the last thing these young parents were interested in was another lecture to pay attention to. Instead they sought conversation with people who shared their life experience and who could offer understanding and support.

When the results of the conversations with the parents were reported to the adult education committee, the committee's first response was . . . "Well, we're going to have to get better speakers for our program."

From a distance, it is easy to see that the response of "better speakers" to attract people who don't want to listen to lectures is a wrong answer. But for our purposes, it is worth exploring how natural the reach for such "wrong answers" is and why clear outcomes and appropriate strategies for effective ministry are so necessary.

1. The propensity to action: Perhaps one of the most difficult hurdles for leaders to manage is the propensity to move to immediate action. When faced with a "problem," the natural inclination of leaders is to move to action—to do something to fix the problem. However, the immediate move from problem to action precludes learning what is new in the situation that might require a different response. This propensity commonly leads to the adage "When people don't know what to do, they do what they know."

2. The power of the "priming effect": In an article by church consultant Jeff Bullock, the work of economist Daniel Kahneman is brought to bear on how congregations make decisions.[1] Kahneman notes the power of the priming effect—that once we have had frequent exposure to a word, concept or number, our thinking is conditioned to recognize that word, concept or number again. "If we read the word 'eat' enough times," writes Bullock, "the next time we see a word that could be read as either soup or soap, we're likely to choose soup." The longer that congregational leaders are exposed to Christian education as the sharing of information and ideas by experts, the more likely the logical fix to a struggling program would seem to be better speakers and better lectures. The leaders were primed to recognize a particular response to their problem, even if they themselves knew that it wouldn't help.

3. The trap of the "focusing illusion": Here again, using Kahneman's work, Bullock points to the dilemma of the focusing illusion—the psychological tendency to "substitute an easier question for a more difficult question when the more difficult question has no immediate or obvious answer." The far easier question for the adult education leaders was how to contact and schedule excellent lecturers for their adult classes. The much more difficult question was how to do Christian formation with young adults who are worried about their families, marriages, careers and the world their children live in, and who want their faith to make a difference in how they live as they manage their concerns. Faced with the difficult question of Christian formation, the adult education leaders easily substituted a more familiar question of Christian education programming for which they already had a known answer.

4. The wish for an easy answer: We do wish for easy answers, for silver bullets, for proven programs, for implementable solutions. When

paradigms shift, when deep change is needed, our very assumptions, values and behaviors are questioned. The real challenge is to
re-invent the very world we live in. However, we have been primed
by an earlier time to expect that leadership is about applying solutions and to expect that committees are about making decisions and
implementing action. We would much prefer the former way in
which someone gives us the answer to our dilemma and lets us go to
work on what we know how to do.

Getting clear about outcomes (intended differences), the subsequent
strategies (the means of achieving intended differences) and the appropriate use of the metrics of measuring is essential to purposeful ministry
and is the subject of this chapter. A congregation must actively set itself to
align with a difference that God dreams of for the corner of the Kingdom
in which the congregation finds itself. Central to the argument is the idea
that a clear, specific, and measurable outcome is necessary to align the
purpose of the church with God's intention. It was the lack of a clear, measurable outcome that confounded the leaders in the Presbyterian example
above and that led leaders down the false path of protecting an established program rather than setting bolder goals of making a difference in
the lives of young adults that would require different strategies of them.

A clear outcome, describing the change the people believe is called
for by God and given to them to achieve, provides a congregation with
purpose and identity that is essential to vitality. Yet the identification and
claiming of clear and measurable outcomes is some of the most difficult
work that leaders of a congregation will do because it involves discernment, making choices, continual learning and boldness. There is more to
the process of discernment than we often acknowledge.

Let's start with counting and measuring again. Recall that both counting and measuring are essential to a congregation but that they are different tools serving different functions in the life and purpose of the congregation (see table 3.1). Let's look at the distinction a bit more closely (*1).

Table 3.1. A Comparison of Counting and Measuring

COUNTING	MEASURING
Focus is on resources and activities— What currently is	Focus is on outcomes—Intended differences of what is not yet
Answers the questions of how many, how often, and how much	Answers the question of how far we have moved toward our intended difference
Indicator of strength, health, potential	Indicator of movement toward the goal
Related to vitality	Related to purpose
Axiomatic and belonging to every congregation/conference	Unique and specific to each congregation/conference

VITAL CONGREGATIONS—
KNOWING WHERE COUNTING FITS IN

I have been referencing the United Methodist Call to Action as an example of a clear denominational initiative to increase the number of vital congregations in the denomination. Initiated by the Council of Bishops, the Call to Action developed a vitality index for United Methodist congregations based on research reported in the Towers and Watson report of June 2010. Key indicators of vitality (such as growth, engagement, involvement, giving) were identified that were used as measures by which 32,288 United Methodist congregations were screened. From the screening, 15 percent of the congregations surfaced as being vital. Further measures and comparisons of this 15 percent of congregations were taken. From a list of more than one hundred ministries and strategies, Towers and Watson found that vital congregations had sixteen variables in common. These sixteen variables were identified as "drivers" of vitality, and they clustered around four central foci of church life and ministry.

The sixteen indicators of congregational vitality were then used to establish a benchmark of vitality, a standard that was then determined to be met by only 15 percent of United Methodist congregations. Much of the denominational focus of the Call to Action has been on increasing the number of vital congregations. Indeed, the adaptive challenge for the denomination is now identified as the need to radically redirect our attention and resources to increase the number of vital congregations, as measured against the benchmarks of the Towers and Watson research. In a variety of ways, the counting related to vital congregations has been at the foundation of most of the annual conference dashboards to which individual congregations report their own data in an ongoing process.

It is worth reviewing the benchmarks from this research and the work of the Council of Bishops' "Team Vital," led by Bishop John Schol of the Greater New Jersey Annual Conference. Through this work we now have a vitality index which identifies the actual metric or percentage that a congregation needs to achieve in order to meet the established benchmark for vitality (*6):[2]

Growth

- On average, U.S. highly vital congregations increase worship attendance by 4 percent over five years. The average worship attendance change for all U.S. churches is -7 percent.
- On average, U.S. highly vital congregations increase the number of professions of faith by 82 percent over five years. The average change in the number of professions of faith for all U.S. churches is -11 percent.

Involvement

- On average, U.S. highly vital congregations have 106 percent of their worship attendance involved in a small group or some ongoing study opportunity. This number may seem inaccurate, but it exceeds 100 percent because the average worship attendance does not include some people who go to small groups, like children in Sunday school or youth in a youth group. The average for all U.S. churches is 5 percent.
- On average, U.S. highly vital congregations have 9 percent of their worship attendance who are young adults involved in study groups that include Bible study, Sunday school and other groups for learning. The average for all U.S. churches is 5 percent.
- On average, U.S. highly vital congregations have 56 percent of their total professing members in average worship attendance. The average for all U.S. churches is 51 percent.

Engaged

- On average, U.S. highly vital congregations have 20 percent of their worship attendance engaged as a volunteer in mission ministry. The average for all U.S. churches is 8 percent.
- On average, U.S. highly vital congregations have 6 percent of their worship attendance that join by profession of faith or are restored in a given year. This does not include confirmands. The average for all U.S. churches is 2 percent.

Giving

- U.S. highly vital congregations give 100 percent of their apportionments for the most current year.
- On average, U.S. highly vital congregations grow mission giving by 12 percent over five years. The average for all U.S. churches is -15 percent.
- On average, U.S. highly vital congregations grow non-capital spending by 22 percent over five years. The average for all U.S. churches is 2 percent over five years.

Given the argument in this book, there are several points to be made about the focus on vital congregations and the use of dashboard counting that is related to directing our denominational attention and resources to increasing the number of vital congregations.

1. The attention to vital congregations is absolutely essential to the mission and ministry of the United Methodist Church. Increasing

the number of vital congregations is not a new institutionalism motivated by a denomination that needs to increase its resource base to sustain the denominational structure and commitments already in place. In fact, the current denominational structure and commitments are very much under scrutiny, with suggestions and experiments at the annual conference and general church levels, for what is needed for a mission-based future. The mission of the United Methodist Church is to make disciples of Jesus Christ and to transform the world. Disciples are made in community, primarily in local congregations. If the United Methodist Church is sincere in its call and commitment to making disciples, more vital congregations to fulfill that mission are quite simply needed. More congregations are needed that have a passion for making disciples, with an awareness of the tools and resources needed for making disciples, and with the vitality to do the work.

2. The vitality index is an invaluable tool of health for all congregations. The vitality index is a benchmark. A benchmark is "a standard or point of reference against which things may be compared or assessed." One of the primary tasks of leadership in all organizations is to first draw an honest picture of the current reality of the organization. If a benchmark of vital congregations is an increase in worship attendance by 4 percent over five years, it is important for leaders of a local congregation to know where they stand in relationship to that benchmark. If their worship attendance has plateaued or declined over the past five years, it raises questions about vitality for the future and the potential for making disciples. Benchmarks very appropriately draw attention to critical issues of health and performance and give feedback to direct future action. Like one's blood pressure, weight or cholesterol, which are all standard benchmarks of health monitored and used to direct action by one's physician, there are benchmarks appropriate to organizations, congregations included. Benchmarks are to be used by leaders to be honest about the current reality, to assess potential and need for change and to direct attention and action toward health and vitality.

3. The focus of the work on vital congregations and the vitality index is appropriately related to resources and activities—it is dependent on counting. Vitality is not an end goal for a congregation: it is a measure of the potential of the congregation for accomplishing the real outcome of ministry, which is making disciples and changing the world. Vitality is a measure of resources and activities—how many people at worship, how many groups, how many involved in mission, how much money? "If one of you wanted to build a tower, wouldn't you first sit down and calculate the cost to determine

whether you have enough money to complete it? . . . Or what king would go to war against another king without first sitting down to consider whether his ten thousand soldiers could go up against the twenty thousand coming against him?" (Luke 14:28, 14:31). Leaders must know who they are, what resources they have and what resources they need for the demands of their future.

4. As a tool of counting, the vitality index belongs to all congregations. A benchmark is a standard against which all related organizations can measure themselves. While the standard may not easily fit all, and while there may be community, demographic or historic reasons for a congregation to be at variance with the standard, nonetheless a benchmark is a standard against which all United Methodist congregations can be measured.

5. The vitality of a congregation is not the same as the purpose of a congregation. Vitality is related to the resources of the congregation and its potential for mission. Purpose is related to the intended outcome of the work and ministry of the congregation and, as such, must be individually determined and must use individually determined measurements of progress toward the intended difference. Getting clear about this distinction is critical to leaders for knowing when to use the tools appropriate to counting and when to use the tools appropriate to measuring.

WHAT THEN? VITALITY FOR WHAT? QUESTIONS THAT PRECEDE MEASURES

If vitality is a counting of resources—indicators of strength and health and potentially applicable to all congregations—the obvious next question is Resources for what? To what are the strength, health and potential of a congregation to be bent? As I have been arguing, for that answer leaders must turn to the work of identifying specific outcomes unique to their individual congregation or annual conference and the use of appropriately developed measures to monitor progress toward that outcome. It is a work of a different order. While counting can be done at any time because of its focus on resources and activities, measuring depends upon there being—and can only be employed if there is—a clear and specific outcome to measure against.

The reality is that any metric that is applied to all congregations or conferences has its limits and is confined to limited use. Mission is global but strategy is local. While the mission of making disciples and transforming the world belongs to all United Methodist annual conferences and congregations, the specific strategy by which that is to be done is determined by the local setting and the local needs. "Pastors cannot readily assume that the assumptions they take into the pulpit, the illustrations they find most meaningful or the sermon forms they most enjoy using will be equally accessible to, or meaningful for, their hearers," writes Professor of Preaching Leonora Tubbs Tisdale. She presents preaching as an act of constructing "local theology—that is, theology crafted for a very particular people in a particular time and place."[3] Whatever the eternal truth of Christ, meaning must be found in the context of the immediate history of a people and the specific questions confronting them as individuals and as community. Whatever the mission of the denomination, the immediate purpose of an annual conference or a local congregation must be framed by the local context and the gap that an annual conference or local congregation experiences between their stated mission and the current internal and external realities being lived. Outcomes must reflect local theology and local mission.

Again, for example, the mission of the United Methodist Church is to make disciples of Jesus Christ for the transformation of the world—a mission that belongs to all. But in the midst of that shared mission, the Greater New Jersey Conference experienced Hurricane Sandy in October 2012, the second-costliest hurricane in U.S. history. Or consider the Western Pennsylvania Conference, which sits in the center of the Marcellus Shale field, or the Dakotas Conference in the Bakken Shale field, or the conferences of Texas, which have four shale fields. With the shared mission for all conferences of making disciples and transforming the world, these annual conferences are all addressing that purpose, but doing so in the context of the health and political questions of fracking; the fallout of "fraccidents"; work-force "man camps" that spring up overnight, stretching communities and human needs to their limits; and the imposition of new wealth on old congregations that have already lost any purpose beyond survival. As I write, there is a newly forming Rio Texas Conference, in the southern half of Texas. It will become a predominantly Anglo institution in a territory in which Hispanics are already more than 50 percent of the population. While it shares a mission with its sister conferences, it must learn to live with feet fully planted in two different "dominant cultures." How to make disciples and change the world is a question that belongs to all of these conferences, but the specific strategies for making disciples and changing the world must be unique to the local setting and measured by the local needs. The better question for each of the conferences is how are they to make disciples and how are they to transform their part of the world given the reality of their setting? The measurable outcomes of each conference must focus on what they specifically need to next put in place in order to get closer to their purpose of making disciples and changing the world.

Consider a small city church, with regional membership, surrounded by at-risk youth in an urban poverty environment. Compare such a church to a suburban congregation with a growing component of young families with dual-income parents who are stressed by the very thin margins of their lives. Or compare these to a county-seat church of white Anglos located in a demographic area quickly growing with people of different ethnic and socioeconomic backgrounds, or a rural congregation with a membership of average age in the seventies that is being surrounded by new construction in which the homes for incoming families will be larger than their church building. If these are all churches of the same denomination, they all share the same mission and all should be very aware of, and attending to, their vitality index—a requirement for all. But their local theologies, their individual outcomes and their specific strategies to move toward making disciples and changing the world that surrounds them must be unique and specific to the corner of the Kingdom of God to which they have been assigned.

"I GO AWAY"—FIGURING OUT WHERE WE ARE

When it comes to the general and universal, the mission, goals and metrics can be equally given to all. It is both appropriate and important for a Council of Bishops, a denominational council, to mount a research initiative to provide uniform guidelines and benchmarks of vitality that can guide congregations to the accomplishment of shared mission. When it comes to the local and unique, however, the mission, goals and metrics need to be determined and decided on in the specificity of the context in which they will be lived. The general can be given to all. The specific we need to figure out for ourselves.

> "But now I go away to the one who sent me," said Jesus to his disciples. "I have much more to say to you, but you can't handle it now. However, when the Spirit of Truth comes, he will guide you in all truth." (John 16:5, 16:12–13)

Discernment means that we will not be told everything. We are a Trinitarian people—Father, Son and Holy Spirit. The Father was disclosed by His Son, the Son was the embodiment for us to see and experience, but the Holy Spirit was given to help us discern the truth of the Father and Son in the daily context of our lives centuries after. Discernment means that we are going to have to figure some things out for ourselves—but not arbitrarily, of course. Discernment is constant dialogue with the Spirit of God for our identity and purpose and in constant dialogue with our unique context for the clear and specific need that we are called to make different in the lives of people and their shared life in community. Within that constant dialogue with the Spirit of God and the needs about us, we need to figure out the next appropriate difference that we are to make in the place where we are located.

PRACTICAL WISDOM—"PHRONESIS"

To help understand discernment, the task of figuring out what is next, let's begin with the notion of "practical wisdom." The subtitle of the book *Practical Wisdom* by Schwartz and Sharpe is *The Right Way to Do the Right Thing*. When it comes to making decisions about the right way and right thing, they note,

> Generally we reach for one of two tools. The first tool is a set of rules and administrative oversight mechanisms that tell people what to do and monitor their performance to make sure they are doing it. The second tool is a set of incentives that encourage good performance by rewarding people for it.[4]

But rules and incentives are not sufficient, they observe. What is left out is the essential wisdom that comes from the specifics facing the individual—practical wisdom, identified as *phronesis* by Aristotle. "Without this missing ingredient, neither rules (no matter how detailed and well monitored) nor incentives (no matter how clever) will be enough to solve the problems we face."[5] Phronesis requires figuring it out for ourselves and making choices.

Plato, Aristotle's teacher, saw wisdom as theoretical and abstract, a gift given only to a few. For contemporary Christians, these few might be the mystics and the great leaders who could, by God's hand, see what others could not. Indeed, many of us still wish for these great few who can tell us what to do and relieve us of the burden of decisions, and who, when proven wrong or insufficient, can be blamed.

Aristotle, in contrast, saw that "our fundamental social practices constantly demanded choices—like when to be loyal to a friend, or how to be fair, or how to confront risk, or when and how to be angry—and that making the right choices demanded wisdom."[6] These are choices no one can make for us. Making choices, practical wisdom, requires the ability to honestly perceive the situation one is in, to have the appropriate feelings or motivations about the situation, to deliberate over what could and should be done and then to act. And such work is to be guided by the *telos* of the situation, Aristotle's word for the purpose or aim of an act.

> The telos of teaching is to educate students; the telos of doctoring is to promote health and relieve suffering; the telos of lawyering is to pursue justice.

Every profession—from banking to social work—has a telos, and those who
excel are those who are able to locate and pursue it.[7]

Staying with the mission of the United Methodist denomination, the
telos of a United Methodist annual conference and a United Methodist
congregation is to make disciples of Jesus Christ for the transformation
of the world. It takes phronesis, practical wisdom, to figure out how
that telos will be given life in the local setting. It takes what the church
calls discernment to honestly perceive the situation one is in, to have the
appropriate feelings or motivations about the situation, to deliberate on
what could and should be done and then to act—all done with an open-
ness and attentiveness to what the Spirit of God is calling for for these
people in this place.

PHRONESIS AS THE PRACTICAL WISDOM OF FAITHFULNESS

How then is a middle judicatory or a local church to name a clear and
specific outcome, an intended difference God intends for a specific people
and place? How do we claim a clear and specific outcome against which
we are willing to measure our progress?

We are accustomed to the linear logic of strategic planning. First we must
figure out where we are now—Point A. Then we decide on where we want
to be—Point B. We then draw the difference between the two points and
make a plan to get from Point A to Point B. Yes, all well and good.

However, the real challenge in the current setting is that for a middle
judicatory or a local congregation to name Point B requires discernment,
courage and boldness. *Clearly and specifically, identifying Point B means
making a choice among an array of possibilities to which we can direct the limited attention and resources available to us at any given time.* Indeed, having
limited attention and resources requires that we make a mission-based
choice. However, our established denominational and congregational
norms make such clear choices difficult. We want everyone to have a
voice. We want full agreement to move ahead. Norms such as these
minimize our boldness because they set us in search of decisions that will
make the most people happy and the fewest people angry. When listening so closely to the opinions and preferences of all the members and
participants, it is very easy to miss the quieter voice of God that calls us to
make a difference that goes beyond institutional preservation or personal
preference. Without a clear missional Point B, the church is reduced to an
institution counting its resources and activities, worrying about money
and members and rewarding tiredness as if the completion of tasks and
programs were the purpose of the church.

A missional Point B is the outcome. It is the intended difference that the people discern God calls them to make in their place and in this time. It is the difference to be achieved over the next three to five years that will be most important to measure progress against; for example,

- a denomination that commits to increasing the percentage of clergy under thirty-five years of age so that new generations in the mission field can be served
- a local church that commits to being the first place that the children and their parents from the school across the street will turn to in times of need
- a denomination that commits to increasing the number of highly vital congregations (using benchmarks) and commits to learning how to measure disciple making
- a local church that commits to making disciples (measured by the number of new professions of faith), to a willingness to forgive offenses (measured by an increase of civility toward others), to an increase in the dependence on scripture to bring understanding to their experience—or other markers of discipleship
- a middle judicatory that commits to five new church starts (traditional new congregations) and three new faith community experiments (nontraditional efforts to reach the unchurched with the relevance of the denomination's theological perspective)
- a local church that commits to serving the youth of their community, measured by the percentage of young people who graduate from high school with clear plans to attend college, to attend a technical school or to enter the military
- a denomination or middle judicatory that commits to _____ [add here your boldest difference that you believe is needed to make your annual conference a fruitful instrument of making disciples and transforming the world]
- a local church that commits to _____ [add here your boldest difference that you believe is needed to make your local church a fruitful instrument of making disciples and transforming the world]

ORGANIC DISCERNMENT

To live into the new wilderness of a changed mission field now asks us to discern outcomes and commitments in a new, and much less orderly, manner. Where we once moved from Point A to Point B with confidence, discerning a clear and fruitful outcome now requires an ongoing act of intuition and learning.

I am intrigued by William Duggan's work on strategic intuition. I will stick with my favorite definition of intuition as "practiced wisdom." However, Duggan goes beyond my simpler definition to describe three forms of intuition.[8]

1. *Ordinary intuition* consists of vague hunches, gut instinct. It is a form of feeling, not thinking. It is shaped by our life experiences, and it can commonly be trusted.
2. The second form of intuition is *expert intuition*. This is a form of rapid thinking that allows us to jump to helpful conclusions because we recognize something familiar. Duggan notes that expert intuition is always fast and only works in familiar situations we have faced before.
3. The third form of intuition is *strategic intuition*, which unlike ordinary intuition is thinking, not feeling and, unlike expert intuition, helps us bring clarity to unknown situations not encountered before. Duggan describes strategic intuition as a flash of insight that cuts through the fog of our mind with a clear and shining thought. It comes from connecting ideas and experiences that are already there but find new form and importance as we put them together with purpose in new ways. However, the flash of insight is the product, not the process, of strategic intuition. Strategic intuition itself is always slow, and it works for new situations, which is when we most need such intuitive insight.

Again, I believe we are being invited into the practice that the early church fathers identified as discernment. We slow down. We pray. We compare our experience to God's purpose using regular reading and study of the scripture. We muse. We empty ourselves intentionally to make room for what is needed that goes beyond what we already know or what we already prefer. We talk with one another. We read books together. We play with new ideas. We look for new metaphors that help us see familiar things in new light. We dream. We wait. We listen. These are all part of the process of strategic intuition and very familiar to our understanding of discernment. And then we are called. This calling is the flash of insight and deep feeling that comes with God's purpose. Our familiar circumstances connect in new ways with our prayers, our conversations and our new learning, and we "see" what it is that we are called to make different. The lessons of discernment from the early church fathers tell us that the journey in the wilderness of a new and different mission field is to be determined much more by strategic intuition than by logical decision making by leaders and committees.

Duggan notes, "[Strategic planning] tells you to pick your desired objective and march toward it . . . [Strategic intuition] tells you to wait for the decisive point when a combination of past examples can achieve a worthy goal."[9] Strategic planning tells you to *control the flow*. Strategic intuition tells you to *go with the flow*. For a people who believe God is already active in our world, it is more appropriate to go with the flow of God's Spirit. We will not control it.

READY—FIRE—AIM: MOVING QUICKLY INTO SLOW DISCERNMENT

Discernment of God's purpose in our lives, in our congregation, in our community is, therefore, a slow and ongoing process of being open and being willing to live with questions. It is not the quick decision making that we so much want from our leaders. On the other hand, we cannot wait. Our time is limited. The United Methodist denomination is now on a trajectory in which some 11,500 congregations may close in the next seventeen years, based on current trends. Within the United Methodist denomination, the average age is twenty-two years older than the national average for all people in the United States—a clear indication that we are now irrelevant to younger generations. For a United Methodist denomination, the greatest strength and attraction remains within the Anglo middle class at a time when our nation is becoming less and less Anglo-centric and the middle class is disappearing into a changed configuration of a new upper class of the educated elite and an exploding new lower class.[10] These descriptors of the United Methodist denomination are not appreciably different from those of other mainline denominations. Indeed, there are now hints that evangelical denominations are beginning to see similar trends of decline that will follow a similar mainline path as they too live into the changed culture.

These few descriptions of current trends offer indisputable evidence that our denomination is unsustainable as it currently is and that we have only a few years to make significant changes. At the same time, discernment of God's purpose and learning how to live in a new mission field is a long, slow and faith-shaping experience. The lesson we must now learn was stated by an experienced brain surgeon standing next to a resident surgeon in training who said, "Now remember, from the time you open the skull you only have three minutes before the patient experiences stress—so work slowly."

The temptation, when we are faced with a strong need to make deep changes that are both correct and quick, is to want to stand at Point A, get a clear sighting of Point B, and just go to work. It is the familiar path of strategic planning: Ready—Aim—Fire. But it only works in a controlled environment when Point B is both known and correct, allowing us to stand at A (Ready), clearly see B (Aim) and thus move to quick action (Fire).

Ours is not a time of Ready—Aim—Fire but rather a time of bold learning that asks of us Ready—Fire—Aim. Ready—Fire—Aim asks us to put action and discernment together.

Consider this new challenge of Ready—Fire—Aim in the example of one person who found an important outcome to be addressed and then had to learn, step by step, how to address it—while doing it. In his earlier professional life, Steve Rothschild launched Yoplait yogurt in the United States and went on to become executive vice president of General Mills. Sometime in the 1980s, working in the Twin Cities area, he became aware of issues of poverty and the barriers facing low-income adults living in generational poverty. Rothschild, after a considerable amount of personal discernment about what was pulling at his spirit and after some necessary homework about the situation he was observing around him, changed his work life and established RISE! (Responsible, Independent, Skilled, Employed) in the Minneapolis–St. Paul metropolitan area of Minnesota. RISE! is a nonprofit dedicated to reducing poverty through job employment. As Rothschild tells his story, he is clear about how he set his hand to the task and then needed to learn, adjust, adapt and change along the way: Ready—Fire—Aim.

"I founded RISE!" he wrote, "in order to combat poverty in the Twin Cities, but before I could do that, I had to learn about poverty in the U.S."[11] He learned that most poverty programs operated on the assumption that once people got started on a path of economic self-sufficiency, they could simply bootstrap their way to success. However, as he explored poverty in America, he learned of the difference between situational poverty (common to immigrants who need to begin life in a new place without employment and with few resources) and generational poverty (in which people, after two or three generations of poverty, emerge with a damaged sense of self-worth that combines with a feeling of entitlement that makes someone else responsible for their situation and in which hopelessness brings them to the conclusion that action on their part will produce no change).

The mission, purpose and metrics of RISE! are straightforward, informed by research and well thought out.

> *Purpose*: To reduce concentrated poverty (generational poverty thrives in concentrated, economically depressed, mostly urban neighborhoods).
> *Mission*: To provide employers with skilled workers, primarily men of color. (RISE! accepts people of both sexes and all races but concentrates on impoverished men as the group underserved by most poverty programs, which are designed to get people off welfare and, therefore, focus on custodial parents who are primarily women.)

Strategy: Provide extensive training in two primary areas: operations (materials handling, warehousing, manufacturing and machine operations) and office support (customer service, clerical work, financial services and call centers).

Outcome and Metrics: The number of graduates who get and keep a living-wage job with benefits for at least two years.

So Rothschild and RISE! got ready—they identified the need and did the necessary homework to be clear about their purpose, mission, strategy, outcome and metrics. They fired—they got their program up and running.

And then they aimed. What is important for our consideration of setting outcomes in the church is that the bulk of the story of RISE! as told in Rothschild's book is about what they learned after they started their work and how it made them adapt and change their strategy, their program, their expectations, their requirements, their assumptions.

- They learned that the participants in their program needed to know a culture of business that was foreign to their experience, so RISE! chose a management structure for their own program that would reflect the structure of the companies in which their participants would find work.
- They learned that the offices of RISE! needed to be designed to replicate the offices of employers in order to accustom their participants to feeling comfortable in their future surroundings.
- They learned to test their participants for drug use, not because many of the participants had a history of alcohol or drug abuse, but because drug testing was part of the culture of most of the employers where RISE! participants would seek employment.
- They learned that while the average length of time for a participant to complete the RISE! program was thirteen months, it could take some people two years or more. RISE! continued to work with a participant for any amount of time necessary, as long as the participant was accountable for his or her work. But RISE! quickly learned that accountability required a positive system of beliefs, feelings and skills from their participants. To accomplish this part of the work required RISE! to move well beyond job training to teach a particular set of cognitive and emotional skills along with a positive belief system.

The current situation of our North American denominations and many of their congregations is that they must boldly act because they have a clear mission and a clear understanding of why they can't wait. But like RISE! they have much to learn as they do their work. We all must learn about making a difference in this new mission field in which we now find ourselves. We all are in the uncomfortable position of Ready—Fire—Aim. Significantly, Rothschild writes about being "learning driven" and notes that for new initiatives, one of the biggest barriers to experiential learning is over-planning! Too much planning delays startup and interferes with learning how to actually accomplish the difference one sets out to make. He notes that the best-laid plans must change frequently, not because the planning was poorly done, but because we can't predict the future and must be prepared to learn from it.

The story of RISE! is inspiring and instructive. However, an undertaking like this is also large, complex and demands resources and a full network of stakeholders. For many middle judicatories and congregations, the story of RISE! will seem like too much to take on. But at its simplest, it is a story about dissatisfaction and discernment (seeing the world as God would have it, not as it is); about action (doing the homework, setting an outcome and getting started); and about shaping the path of mission as one goes (being willing to question results and learn from what does and does not work). Ready—Fire—Aim.

Reduced to these simpler principles, clear outcomes of ministry that make a measurable difference are well within the reach of any congregation or conference. A favorite example from noted consultant Lyle Schaller is a very small family church that questioned its purpose and connected it to a young child in one of the families of the church who was physically challenged and attended a special school that could accommodate his needs. They connected the fact that they knew how to throw a birthday party to their realization that Bobby, this young boy, had never been invited to a birthday party. So they decided to make a clear difference, and they threw a birthday party for Bobby, encouraging him to invite his friends from his special school, who also never got invited to birthday parties. They learned that special needs children can't participate in many things without a parent's presence, and they ended up with a real celebration of children and parents, all needing support. The party was so good that the church determined to have another birthday party the following month, since surely it would be someone's birthday. This time the children who attended Bobby's party were encouraged to invite their friends (and subsequently those friends' parents). Quickly the church learned to build a bridge to its surrounding community. Having taken their first shot with Bobby's birthday party, they learned how to aim higher at making a difference in the lives of their full community. In the process, their own spirits were changed.

Disappointingly, it is fairly common to see many congregations short-circuit their mission by practicing Ready—Fire—Quit. For example, one midsize urban congregation in Pennsylvania that I worked with determined that they had lost their connection with the community they lived in. All of their members now drove to church, and almost no one from the neighborhood participated in the church. They planned a street fair—a very public event of games, music and food by which they intended to get to know their neighbors. (Ready.) The day came, after much effort and considerable use of resources, and they set up their fair. (Fire.) And no one from the neighborhood came. The disappointment was palpable, and they began to argue with one another about what went wrong. (Quit.) A short time later, I was called to help them manage their argument. As I asked about their fair, I discovered that the primary way in which they had advertised the fair and invited their neighbors was through announcements from the pulpit. They were angry at their neighbors for not attending a fair that the neighbors didn't even know about. A rookie mistake, to be sure. However, had they been willing to learn, instead of fighting, they could have easily re-aimed for their next shot. Instead, they quit because of their unwillingness to learn from their first attempt and their lack of courage to try again to move toward a missional future.

THE METRICS OF MEASUREMENT— HOW FAR HAVE WE COME?

It is here, at the intersection between an established outcome (providing graduates from RISE! who will get and keep a living-wage job with benefits for at least two years) and the continual learning and adapting that RISE! had to do to be successful in their mission, that the metrics of measurement belong. "How far have we moved toward our outcome?" This was the question that the church with the street fair desperately needed to ask. This is the question that measures achievement and progress but which also asks about next steps and what needs to be learned and tried next.

It is similar to "performance management" in supervision. Performance management is a tool of supervision in an organization in which the supervisor regularly engages the person being supervised in a learning conversation about how far the person is progressing in their work toward expected outcomes. It is a regular conversation conducted monthly or bi-monthly that does not look at what went wrong but at what has happened so far and what needs to happen next. In our book on staffing and supervision in large congregations, Susan Beaumont and I offered a typical agenda of a performance management meeting.[12]

The Agenda

1. A review of the past month (or two months):

   - What actions have you taken? These should be the details of performance since the last performance management meeting.

- What discoveries have you made? This should be an account of formal and informal learning done since the last performance management meeting. What are the new insights, and from where did they come?
- What partnerships have you built? What new relationships have been built, or what old relationships have been strengthened?

2. A forecast for the next time period:

- What is your main focus now? What are the primary goals that will get your priority attention over the next month or months?
- What are you planning to learn over the next month or months?
- What new partnerships (new relationships or strengthening of old relationships) are you hoping to build over the next month or months?

The practice of performance management acknowledges that at each step, our efforts will naturally lead to new learning and the identification of additional steps. It also acknowledges that we don't do our work alone, that we must build relationships and coalitions to progress toward our outcome. In the next chapter we will turn our attention to some of the actual measurement tools related to outcomes that can help the ongoing learning and development of our work toward the outcome that God calls us to. But note for the time being that, like performance management, using the metrics of measurement does not evaluate our success (+/-) but enables us to locate where we are so far in our work and where we need to go next.

GETTING TO OUR OUTCOME

Our natural default position is to think of an outcome as an answer—we assume that deciding what difference we are to make will solve our problem or answer our question. It feels as if A should lead directly to B. Fruitfulness of mission and ministry is much more dynamic than that. First steps lead naturally to second steps, even if not anticipated. Questions wrestled with commonly lead to better questions. The value of the metrics of measuring is in constantly asking "how far" we have moved toward making the difference we are called to make. The constant asking of "how far" will teach us, guide us and embolden us to more and more ministry, more and more fruitfulness and more and more relevance to a world that wonders whether the church makes any difference at all. Getting to our outcome is commonly not a straight path of making a decision and then acting. Rather, getting to our outcome is a continual process set by boldness and a belief in God's difference in our world followed by ongoing conversation and discernment marked by action, measurements and learning. The nature or shape of an ongoing outcome conversation may be thought of as follows (*7).

1. Question God's purpose for your church or conference for the next three to five years.
2. Dream big. Be bold about what you can make different because it moves you closer to fruitfulness in your purpose.
3. Commit to making a difference in the lives of people or your community, and name the difference, describing it as deeply as you can.
4. See how. Ask what other churches or conferences know about achieving your outcome. Search the literature. Use your own experience to learn next steps.
5. Work hard.
6. Measure results. Constantly track how far you have come in getting to your outcome.
7. Repeat again, starting with step number 3.

READY—FIRE—AIM

As noted, all nonprofit organizations find it difficult to set clear, measurable outcomes. It is hard to work our way from the ideal for which we exist to the necessary proximate steps we need to take in order to actually move toward that ideal. It is one thing to know our mission. It is quite a different matter to discern what is required first and then subsequent steps must be put in place in order to move us closer to that central purpose.

As leaders, it is important for us to understand that discerning God's outcome for our congregation or conference in our "particular corner of the Kingdom" in which we have been placed is a path fraught with distractions and emotions. In the midst of this project on metrics, the Texas Methodist Foundation hosted a gathering of about forty leaders from across the United States to explore the issues of metrics and outcomes. As a part of the day's work, the group developed a "force-field analysis," a mapping of the drivers that help us move toward clear outcomes and of the resisters that block our path to getting clear about God's dream for us. The list of resisters was very telling. As you begin the outcome conversation as outlined above, consider the many issues and reactions that may easily get in the way of clarity. A partial list of the resisters identified by the group includes the following.

- We resist a self-awareness that may indicate we are not doing what we are called to do.
- We don't know the Gospel stories well enough to compel us to action.

- We suffer from the "tyranny of the urgent"—there are so many things we need to care for.
- We live with a theology of scarcity—aware of what we lack, not of what we can do.
- We are tired already, and a call to new work is too much.
- We lack opportunities to collaborate and to unite with others in purpose.
- We are faced with required new learning, and we don't know how to learn.
- We, quite frankly, like it the way it is, and a clear outcome identifying a needed difference may work against our own satisfaction and preferences.
- We might need to change. If we go down this path, it might require some personal change in our own lives.

When we're using the old strategic planning assumptions of moving from Point A to Point B, the variety of resisters named above will seem like a host of problems, all needing solutions in order for us to move ahead to a clear decision about God's outcome for our congregation or conference. However, when we're approaching our leadership as an act of discernment, it becomes easier to see the list above as a potential agenda for work, conversation and learning that will bring us closer to God's call for our lives, our congregation, our conference. We don't have time to solve all of the problems we face before we begin. As a church, as Christian community, we are currently unsustainable as we are. We must begin, and learn as we go.

So . . . Ready—Fire—Aim. Get started. Ask the question of what purpose God has for you that will make a clear difference in the lives of people and in your community. Set an outcome that will make a difference that is both important and needed. Take some steps. It may take you to Bible study to connect Gospel stories that are meant to compel you to action. It may make you confront your own anxiety of scarcity in which we never seem to feel that we have enough while living in the midst of the richest consumer society on the globe. It may require you to reach out to other congregations or middle judicatories to learn from the experience of those who have already gone ahead. Measure your progress. Learn what you need to do next.

Dealing with these natural resisters is not a barrier to fruitfulness. Rather, these are steps of discipleship—of learning how to be disciples and learning how to change the world. These are the conversations leading to the clear purpose and measurable differences that disciples of Jesus Christ are meant to have.

FOUR

Counts, Measures and Conversations: Using New Tools for Fruitfulness

Metrics is about more than numbers and the attendant charts, graphs and statistics that can come from numbers. We North Americans are deeply marinated in Western European Enlightenment assumptions about the capacity to count and control everything through the sciences and rational logic. We believe in numbers. Numbers give solidity and concreteness to our conversations and thinking. Numbers validate our actions and decisions. We regularly turn to numbers to give our actions direction. All of this is done, perhaps, to excess. A long favorite joke about statistics is "Did you know that 48.6 percent of all statistics are made up?" Like all humor, there is some truth in the jest. We so believe in numbers that when we find ourselves lacking them, we invent them. However, numbers, as well as our dependence on them, also have their limits.

In a February 2013 column in the *New York Times*, David Brooks tells the story of a chief executive of a large bank who had to decide if his bank should pull out of investments in Italy because of the weak economy and impending euro crisis.[1] The CEO knew the numbers involved, all of which indicated growing risk. However, the CEO ultimately decided to maintain his bank's investments in Italy. As Brooks noted, the CEO made his decision on the basis of values, not numbers. He did not want his Italian colleagues to think his bank was a fair-weather friend that was unwilling to ride out a potential crisis, even with short-term costs. He understood that the value of trust could exceed the value of numbers. Brooks went on to identify a number of areas where data struggles and provides less than we need. For example, he noted that "data struggles with the social." Numbers offer little information to help us read the emotions and understand the behavior of others. Similarly, data does not do well in understanding context. The stories we tell often do better than numbers at navigating the multiple causes and contexts of our experience. And given the thesis of this book, I might add that data, by itself, can operate without purpose. Data has the power to direct action that may or may not lead us to the end we seek. All of which suggests that in our work on metrics, we need to be able to orient ourselves in the midst of the numbers that we use if we are going to move our congregations and conferences toward fruitfulness.

FROM DATA TO KNOWLEDGE— FROM COUNTING TO MEASURING

In the transition over the past decades from a manufacturing economy to an information economy, one of the organizational disciplines that has developed is "knowledge management." Attention to the new stature and use of information has been an important part of our shift into an information economy. Above all else, what we have learned from this new discipline affirms the need for conversation and discernment about our "counting" before we can approach measures of fruitfulness.

Let's begin with basic definitions—the differences between data, information and knowledge. In their book on organizational management of knowledge, Davenport and Prusak offer the following definitions.[2]

- *Data* is a set of discrete, objective facts about events. In an organizational context, data is most usefully described as structured records of transactions.
- *Information* is . . . a message. As with any message, it has a sender and a receiver. Information is meant to change the way the receiver perceives something, to have an impact on his judgment and behavior. It must inform; it's data that makes a difference.
- *Knowledge* is a fluid mix of framed experience, values, contextual information and expert insight that provides a framework for evaluating and incorporating new experiences and information.

Given this conversation about metrics in the church, data is the product of counting resources and activities. It is the simplest form of "discrete, objective facts"—structured records of transactions to be used for some further purpose. The issue central to fruitfulness of our ministry and purpose is how we move from the basic data of our statistical reports and benchmark counts to missional knowledge. How do we move from knowing how many and how much we have to understanding how to be healthy, purposeful and fruitful? Davenport and Prusak assert that it takes intentional work to get from data to knowledge, work they identify through a number of Cs. We transform data into information by adding value through contextualizing, categorizing, calculating, correcting and condensing. In other words, we have to do additional work with the discrete, objective facts of data in order to understand the way in which the data should direct our judgment and behavior. It isn't enough to know our Call to Action benchmark numbers. We need to contextualize, categorize and otherwise work with those numbers. Similarly, moving from information to knowledge requires additional Cs: comparing, discerning consequences, connecting and conversing.

All of this underlines, again, that it is all well and good, even essential, that leaders in the church count. We must know what we have to work with. We must know how we compare to benchmark standards. We need records, trends and dashboards. And we need data about our communities and our world. But then we need to be bold in aligning ourselves with the difference God dreams of for us, for our communities and for our world. From there we measure our way toward fruitfulness by working with our data (through contextualizing, categorizing, calculating, correcting, condensing, comparing, discerning consequences, connecting and conversing) and working with our experience to move toward knowledge—discerning what we are to do and learning how to do it fruitfully.

EXPANDING BEYOND THE COUNTABLES

Perhaps the most difficult work of using metrics is to move beyond the numbers (the quantifiables) to the measures (the qualitatives) of "informativeness and usefulness."[3] Learning to measure beyond easy numbers is a challenge that must be addressed well beyond the church. In an update from the Lewis Center for Church Leadership, Lovett Weems noted,

> Church leaders may think that leading in the business world is so much simpler than in the church since there is one "bottom line" and financial measures give business leaders all they need to know about how they are doing. Not so. A recent survey of global business leaders found that 75 percent say they need better non-financial measures. They admit struggling with inadequate metrics to deal with important components of their work not captured in dollars and cents.[4]

The more one wrestles with the purpose of an organization, the more complex and difficult is the issue of measuring progress and fruitfulness.

Before looking at churches and conferences, let's turn again to art museums to examine the challenge. In a 2004 paper commissioned by the Getty Leadership Institute, Maxwell Anderson, research affiliate of the Center for Arts and Cultural Policy Studies at Princeton University, addresses the metrics of success in art museums.[5] He observes that, increasingly, the boards of art museums disagree about their priorities, which raises fundamental questions about the metrics they are to use in assessing whether an art museum is fulfilling its goals. There was once a consensus that an art museum fulfilled its core purpose by housing a collection of art. This definition of purpose lent itself to straightforward and easily quantifiable measures: the number of items collected, the square footage of viewing space for the public and the number of visitors to view the collection. These are, in fact, all quantifiables, easily counted and connected to resources and activities. Anderson, however, points out that basic assumptions about the purpose of an art museum have changed: "Over the last generation, art museums have shifted their focus away from collection-building and toward various kinds of attention to the public."[6] The conversation among museum boards began to question how museums could have a positive impact on an audience and what "outcomes" would be important to museums.

This is where the wrestling within the community of museums parallels the current conversation in the church. Museums were faced with a shift in which museums had to "compete with each other not for the best exhibitions and the highest attendance but, rather, to 'make a difference.'" This is not unlike the challenge in the mainline church that is facing the shift from making members (collections of people belonging to an institution) to making disciples (people experiencing a "difference" in their lives because of their connection with Christ). Interestingly, Anderson immediately states that "while [making a difference] is a worthy goal, in order to get there we first need to give art museum leaders the tools to measure such outcomes—as well as the steps they must take to achieve them. Without such tools, directors will continue to be rewarded only for excelling in conventional activities . . . as opposed to outcomes."[7]

In fact, the shift from the easy measures of activities to the much more complex measures of outcomes is exactly the conversation sought for the church in this book. At this point, we are challenged to learn new ways that will require creativity. Consider the list of new metrics Anderson identifies for museums that want to be serious about "making a difference."

- quality of experience
- fulfillment of educational mandate
- institutional reputation
- management priorities and achievements
- caliber and diversity of staff
- standards of governance
- scope and quality of collection
- contributions to scholarship
- contributions to art conservation
- quality of exhibitions
- facilities' contribution to core mission

While far from the easy counts of the number of items in a collection, square footage or number of visitors, these new metrics, Anderson suggests, are very different but are, in fact, measurable. The new metrics, however, will require a creativity and inventiveness to build new tools and new conversations to measure progress toward the difference a museum is to make.

The story of leadership in art museums closely parallels the current story about leadership in congregations and annual conferences. It is no longer sufficient to count only dollars and people ("nickels and noses" as one bishop refers to current denominational benchmarks); we must now devise new metrics and then build the tools needed for the new measures. This task will take quite a bit of experimentation and creativity.

As one example, consider a working proposal for assessing annual conference faithfulness and fruitfulness offered by Bishop Mike Lowry of the Central Texas United Methodist Conference.[8] Bishop Lowry proposes two different kinds of categories to be measured:

1. Vital Signs of Faithfulness and Fruitfulness (In this category Bishop Lowry notes sixteen countable metrics of resources and activities that are either simple measures of strength and capacity or measures of variables related to vitality. These metrics are highly related to the Call to Action benchmarks about vitality [*6].)
2. Quality of Life Demonstrating Faithfulness and Fruitfulness

It is in this second category where, as in the work needed by art museums intent on making a difference, new outcomes and new metrics of purposefulness are needed. Consider the metrics suggested for this second category and how new tools will need to be developed to measure progress.

- developing principle-centered Christian leaders
- creating new churches for new people in new places and transforming existing congregations
- working with the poor to eliminate poverty

Beyond the hard numbers of what's easily countable (which satisfy category 1), we must learn to walk into the less quantifiable but necessary measures that will enable us to monitor progress in areas of purpose and values (category 2).

A similar congregational example was offered in chapter 3. Remember that an outcome is defined as the difference a congregation believes it is called by God to make over the next chapter of its life (three to five years). The example of an outcome of a congregation offered in chapter 3 was a local church that commits to making disciples (measured by the number of new professions of faith) or measured by an increase of civility toward others, a willingness to forgive offenses, an increase in the dependence on scripture to bring understanding to one's experience.

On the one hand, part of this outcome is easily counted. The number of professions of faith is easily countable and found in a congregation's annual statistical record. However, while making a profession of faith is a step toward discipleship, it is not the full measure of discipleship. There are other aspects of discipleship, as suggested in this example, such as civility toward others, the capacity to offer forgiveness and incorporation of scripture in understanding life experience. The particular aspects of discipleship to receive attention depend upon what is most needed in a particular congregation. These differences, however, are also measurable. The dilemma is that these differences are of a different order than counting the number of people who have made a discrete decision. A different order of outcomes will require new tools and strategies to measure.

FROM COUNTING TO DESCRIBING

As he turned his attention from for-profit companies to nonprofit organizations, business consultant Jim Collins was clear that nonprofits do not need to behave more like a business—a poorly ascribed prescription given to too many congregations by frustrated laity familiar with business practices. Instead of nonprofits behaving more like a business, Collins suggests that what is needed is for both businesses and nonprofits to behave with more discipline. The need for discipline does not disappear simply because an organization does not operate according to financial measures. Collins refers to nonprofits as organizations of the "social sectors."

In the social sectors, the critical question is not "How much money do we make per dollar of invested capital?" but "How effectively do we deliver on our mission and make a distinctive impact, relative to our resources?" What if your outputs are inherently not measureable? The basic idea is still the same: separate inputs from outputs, and hold yourself accountable for progress in outputs, even if those outputs defy measurement.[9]

Collins insists that it doesn't really matter whether an organization can quantify its results. *What matters is that the leaders continuously and intentionally assemble evidence, quantitative or qualitative, to track progress toward the identified results.* Measuring progress toward a necessary result that cannot be quantified requires that the result be as fully and deeply described as possible. For example, if an annual conference is to be faithful and fruitful (an inherently nonquantifiable result), then faithfulness and fruitfulness must be as richly described as possible. Without a clear description, it is not possible to measure if progress toward the goal is being made. In the example above from the Central Texas Conference, the nonquantifiable outcomes are quality-of-life issues such as developing "principle-centered Christian leaders," "creating new churches for new people in new places and transforming existing congregations" and the elimination of poverty. To assemble evidence of movement toward achieving the quality-of-life issues in category 2, clearer descriptions must be developed about what each of these issues is to look like in the future. What do "principle-centered Christian leaders" look like? What would the elimination of poverty look like in this place, at this time?

Likewise, in the example of the congregation above, once the output of making disciples moves beyond counting the number of new professions of faith in any given year, then much deeper and richer descriptions of discipleship must kick in which define the specifics of discipleship (such as civility, forgiveness or use of scripture). In both the case of the conference and the congregation, once the intended result is richly described, evidence can be collected, and measurements can be made to undergird conversations of leaders learning how to make the difference they believe themselves called to make.

TOOLS FOR THE CONVERSATION

There are already established ways to measure progress toward intended change that can be adapted and used in our quest for fruitfulness. We now turn our attention to a variety of these tools for measuring progress toward well-described but less-quantifiable outcomes. In this section a number of such measurement tools or strategies will be described.

1. Apgar scores
2. Self-report Likert scales
3. Logic models
4. Narrative results mapping

These are tools much less familiar to congregational and conference leaders than the act of counting. But as I have argued from the beginning, new tools are a necessary part of our leadership into a changed mission field that requires our willingness to experiment and learn. To that end, a few things must be said before describing the tools and strategies.

First, what is offered in this section are descriptions of basic models of tools and strategies of measurement. In a number of cases, suggestions for use and examples of how they have been used in congregations or conferences will be offered. However, like all basic models, they need to be adapted and tested for the specific situation in which they will be used. Creativity and experimentation must be the order of the day. The more that leaders use, adapt and share their experience with these tools, and others like them, the better they will serve us in our quest for fruitfulness.

The second guide is that what is offered is not a complete list of tools and strategies. This list is one that focuses on what is easily accessible to congregations and conferences. Others will know of, and will have used, other tools and models. The more we share our experiments and experience of measuring, the more we will complete the tools needed for our leadership toolkit and the more we will become practiced in measuring.

The final point to be recognized is that these are tools and strategies *designed to support conversations of discernment and strategy.* Unlike the quantifiable counts of congregational vitality discussed above, these new measures cannot be connected to benchmarks. There are no universal standards to measure against. In fact, these measures, unlike counts, are specifically designed for use in conversations assessing progress toward unique and specific outcomes. They answer the questions Have we moved closer to our goal? What have we learned that will point to where we need to focus next? and What have we taught ourselves about what we've accomplished already? Less important as reports of success or failure, these measures are critical for learning and discerning conversations among leaders. Like the Israelites, who did not follow a map in the wilderness but made the map of the wilderness, leaders need to continually track progress in order to plan the next steps.

Apgar Scores (*8)

The 1980s in the United States were a time in which manufacturing and service organizations focused intensely on quality as a way of competing in an increasingly aggressive and demanding marketplace. Systems were built with an eye toward reducing manufacturing mistakes and increasing customer friendliness. Quality was broken down into complex components to which managers were to give attention. Programs were developed to increase quality. And to our purpose, arguments ensued about how to measure quality. In the midst of the burgeoning resources and arguments on quality, John Guaspari wrote "a modern fable" about quality in a small book with a title that brought much of the conversation back to a commonsense level: *I Know It When I See It.*[10]

There are times and circumstances in which our counting must give way to the attention that will enable us to quickly and easily see progress toward the difference we are trying to make. Simple and immediate measures can sometimes offer the focus we need to determine right away where we need to give more attention to something or whether or not we are headed in the right direction. We know it because we see it.

Such is the story of the Apgar score, named after Dr. Virginia Apgar, the first woman to be admitted to the surgical residency at Columbia University College of Physicians and Surgeons in 1933. In the mid-1930s, delivering a child was the single most dangerous event in a woman's life, with 1 in 150 births resulting in the mother's death. The situation was even more dire for newborns, with 1 birth in 30 ending in the child's death. In childbirth there is little time for the complex tests of modern medicine, and in the 1930s, 1940s and 1950s, there was much less technology available to offer any tests, even if time permitted. Nonetheless, doctors and nurses needed to know if a newly born child was healthy or needed special care. To meet that need for information, Dr. Apgar developed a simple 0 to 10 score that enabled nurses to rate the condition of babies at birth from simple observation.

- two points if the baby is pink all over
- two points for crying
- two points for taking good vigorous breaths
- two points for moving all limbs
- two points if the heart rate is over a hundred

The baby's condition was easily rated: the nurse would know it when she saw it. The score was taken by a nurse one minute after birth and then again five minutes after birth. A full ten points meant the baby was born in healthy condition; four points or less indicated the baby needed immediate attention. "The Apgar score changed everything. It was practical and easy to calculate, and it gave clinicians at the bedside immediate feedback on how effective their care was."[11]

Apgar-type scores are easily developed for congregational conversations to track progress toward a future the church feels called to live. One of my favorite congregational consultations in the 1990s was in an Episcopal church on the east coast in which the board members regularly fought at church vestry meetings but claimed to really like one another. The fighting was most intense around budget time when decisions had to be made about the use of money. Some on the board argued that any additional dollars above fixed expenses should be used for property maintenance and improvement to care for their facilities. Others on the board argued that any additional dollars above fixed expenses had to be used for mission trips and program staff to make a difference in the spiritual lives of the people who participated in the church. As in most such cases, both sides were right. There were significant needs and opportunities in both of these areas.

In the midst of the consultation, I asked the leaders to determine what biblical story their church was currently living. Finding a church's biblical story is often a powerful way to determine the issues that a faith community is struggling with.[12] Without a great deal of difficulty, the leaders came back with a response well worth talking about. They pointed to the story of Mary and Martha in the Gospel of Luke when, during a visit from Jesus, each of the sisters responds in very different ways. Mary sits at the feet of Jesus and listens to him talk. Martha worries and busies herself with the work in the kitchen until finally she comes to Jesus with her complaint: "Lord, don't you care that my sister has left me to prepare the table all by myself? Tell her to help me" (Luke 10:38–42). "That's us," claimed the leaders of the vestry. "Some of us are worried about the dishes [caring for the facility] while others want to go talk with Jesus [the mission trips and program staff for shaping people's lives]."

After a considerable amount of agreement, which included laughter and the delight of seeing themselves in a new way, the leaders set a goal. Their goal for the next twelve months was that at every vestry meeting, the agenda would reflect both Mary and Martha. They committed themselves to work together, collaboratively instead of competitively, on the agendas of both Martha (the management and maintenance of the church) as well as Mary (the shaping of the lives of the members of the church). It was a commitment to develop their own spiritual leadership.

With a simple "Apgar scale" of board leadership, this group could easily and quickly take continuous measures toward their outcome of modeling spiritual maturity as church leaders (see table 4.1).

Table 4.1.   Scale of Board Leadership

Honoring "Martha" (church management and maintenance) and "Mary" (the development of people's spiritual lives)	
Rate each of the following statements by placing after each statement a number from 0 ("Not at all.") to 2 ("Yes, we did.") based on your experience at this meeting.	Nos. 0 to 2
1. We honored both Martha and Mary by giving attention to each in our meeting.	No._____
2. We collaborated in our work rather than competed for attention and resources.	No._____
3. We treated one another with respect and cared for our relationships as we worked.	No._____
4. We listened to each other, seeking to understand.	No._____
5. Our work focused on the future of our ministry rather than on the past.	No._____
TOTAL:	_____

With a simple measuring tool such as in table 4.1, the leaders of this congregation could keep track of their progress toward the balance of being a church that is both well managed as well as a church that challenges its people to grow in their spiritual lives. Asking board members at the end of a vestry meeting to simply fill out the scale (anonymously, without signing the scale) and hand in their paper for quick collating along with the response of others could give the board immediate feedback on its performance. A score of ten would indicate they were on the right track. A score of six or less would suggest they should look again at their agendas and how they work with one another. In the case of a low score, responses to each of the five individual statements could be reviewed to see which part of their work they needed to give attention to.

Apgar scores are simple tools that are easily constructed and provide a way to measure progress toward a commitment made for the future. Such scores

1. Remind us of what we have said that is important and of commitments we have made;
2. Break our commitments down into simple, observable behaviors— we know it when we see it;
3. Measure our progress, giving immediate feedback to leaders;
4. Are adaptable if we learn that the behaviors we need to give attention to are different from those we determined at the beginning; and
5. Offer suggestions for next steps (telling us to keep going if the ratings are strong or telling us to slow down and look again at what we are doing if the ratings are weak).

Self-Report Likert Scales (*9)

Likert scales are self-report instruments named after American educator and organizational psychologist Rensis Likert. Likert was best known for his research on organizational management styles. A Likert scale is a "psychometric" instrument. It measures knowledge, abilities, attitudes or personality traits by offering scaling responses in survey style. It provides a means for capturing variation. We have all used these scales in a variety of settings, and the basic form below should look familiar.

To what extent have I/we _____ [insert the behavior to be observed and measured]:

1   2   3   4   5

A Likert scale is simply a statement which the respondent is asked to evaluate according to any kind of subjective or objective criteria determined by the respondent. As such, it is a "self-report" instrument—it reports on our own perceptions and judgments and, therefore, is subject to a number of distortions such as central tendency bias, acquiescence bias or social desirability bias. Nonetheless, it is an invaluable tool of direct feedback, making our perceptions and judgments transparent to us in a way that allows for conversation and decision making.

Let's look at three examples of uses of Likert scales in the church:

- feedback on community life
- feedback on personal change
- feedback on alignment with values

FEEDBACK ON COMMUNITY LIFE

Likert scales can be very helpful in congregational or middle judicatory surveys. However, a note of warning before proceeding. Surveys have most commonly been used poorly in the church in two ways: in seeking information about participant preferences; and in seeking to side-step leadership decisions by looking for consensus.

Surveys are problematic when they seek information about preferences (e.g., What kind of church music do you most enjoy? Does the preaching in our church meet your needs?). Preferential surveys invite conflict and subvert mission. When people are asked about preferences, and when people register their preferences, they have a reasonable expectation that their preferences will be followed. Surveys tend to simply measure the differences that are held in a congregation and set people into win/lose categories around their preferences. Such surveys subvert mission because they focus on what people prefer for themselves rather than what is required in order to accomplish a missional outcome.

Similarly, surveys used to side-step decision making (e.g., What time should the new contemporary service be held on Sunday? Should our church hire a part-time youth worker?) divide the community into competing factions. Decisions belong to leadership and should be made on the basis of purpose and outcomes, not on survey results. Being able to offer a clear, missional reason for why the time of a worship service will change or why a part-time youth worker will be hired will garner more support by helping people see the bigger picture than will a testing of consensus to see which is the safer path to take.

That being said, a survey of participants in a church or a conference can be a very helpful tool when it seeks to measure nonquantifiable variables of importance to the mission of the church. For example, in chapter 2 I noted a study on church growth by the Hartford Institute for Religion

Research published by C. Kirk Hadaway.[13] This 2010 survey identifies a number of issues and variables critical to congregations who see their mission as connecting to their mission field and reaching out to new people through church growth. However, unlike the metrics of the Call to Action, these variables are not easily quantifiable. Vitality of worship, clarity of mission and purpose, and congregational identity are three variables critical for growth that, while not subject to counting, can be measured. The use of a Likert scale in these areas can provide church or conference leaders with valuable information about how these variables are currently perceived in the congregation. Such information offers help in determining where leaders should put their attention and effort in order to connect themselves to the mission field. Consider the Likert scale in table 4.2, developed using the information from the Growth 2010 research study, which would provide measures in these key areas.

Each of the statements in table 4.2 is based on findings from the Growth 2010 research. The Growth 2010 report indicates that one of the stronger correlates of growth is the extent to which a congregation has a clear mission and purpose. In the area of congregational identity, the report indicates that the level of growth is greatest on the two ends of the theological spectrum: very liberal and very conservative. This suggests that a clear theological identity may be a descriptor of vitality. It would be very helpful to pastors and leaders to know what, if any, theological identity their congregation claims. The report identified a number of descriptors of worship that correlate with growth (numbers 8, 9 and 10 in table 4.2 correlate very strongly with growth; numbers 11 and 12 correlate less strongly). Rather than asking people their preferences in worship, consider how much more helpful it would be to leaders if they had an idea of how people perceived their current worship, as described by characteristics deemed significant by research. Consider how helpful to purposeful conversation it would be if leaders of a church read the Growth 2010 report together and simultaneously measured where their own congregation perceived itself to be on a scale of the variables identified in the report.

Such nonquantifiable measures can enable leaders to identify issues and variables of their community life that are known to be important but that need attention and development for vitality and effectiveness. Consider the potential for leaders to receive the feedback on a scale such as in table 4.2 from everyone who attends worship on a Sunday morning. Consider, further, the opportunity of asking your thirty newest members/participants to complete the scale separately so that their composite scores can be compared to long-time members/participants to test if long-time and short-time participants have a shared or differing perspective.

Table 4.2. The Likert Scale

A Survey on Our Church

Directions: Please circle the number on each scale that most represents your personal agreement or disagreement with each statement.

1 = strongly disagree   4 = agree
2 = disagree   5 = strongly agree
3 = neither agree nor disagree

Purpose and Missional Clarity:

1. Our church has a clear mission and purpose.

   1   2   3   4   5

2. Our church is spiritually vital and alive.

   1   2   3   4   5

3. Our church is a "moral beacon" in our community.

   1   2   3   4   5

4. We are different from other churches in our community.

   1   2   3   4   5

Our Theological Identity:

5. Our church is theologically conservative.

   1   2   3   4   5

6. Our church is theologically liberal.

   1   2   3   4   5

7. Our church has no clear theological identity.

   1   2   3   4   5

Our Worship is:

8. Joyful

   1   2   3   4   5

9. Innovative

   1   2   3   4   5

10. Inspirational

   1   2   3   4   5

11. Thought provoking

   1   2   3   4   5

12. Filled with a sense of God's presence

   1   2   3   4   5

FEEDBACK ON PERSONAL CHANGE

A primary task of a congregation is to shape people as disciples of Christ, to change people's lives. The example used several times in these chapters is a congregation that has determined that the outcome needed in their individual church is to influence people's civility, their capacity for forgiveness and their use of the discipline of scripture reading and study to bring perspective and meaning to their experience. In a congregation that has a history of conflict, gossip, holding grudges and self-absorption, a decision by church leaders to address these particular practices of discipleship would be more than reasonable. The pastor might intentionally plan worship and sermons to address these themes. The church could name a theme that would highlight discipleship and these specific practices as important in the life of the church. Adult education leaders could seek resources to focus on these issues of Christian life. Small groups could be asked to address these issues in their meetings.

Contrary to many people's assumptions, changes in such areas in a person can be measured if one allows for self-report information that can come from a Likert Scale (see table 4.3).

The development and use of such a tool serves multiple purposes. It

- helps clarify for leaders, members and participants what discipleship specifically means at the present moment in a particular congregation
- describes the intended outcome of the ministry of a specific church very richly and deeply at a behavioral level
- provides leaders with the opportunity to have conversations around whether their church is making a difference in the lives of its members and participants

In addition, asking people to complete the scale a second time six months later can give evidence of whether the worship, preaching, teaching and modeling of leaders is moving the church toward the outcomes identified. It can offer evidence of whether people's lives are being changed or not. It can further identify if any one or more of the identified behavioral disciplines needs more attention than the others.

FEEDBACK ON ALIGNMENT WITH VALUES

One of the key ways in which leaders must measure their own work is the extent to which they are actually behaving in ways they believe they must in order to produce the difference they are called to address. The change required in many congregations and conferences goes well beyond decisions about programs or simple next steps. The change

Table 4.3. Example of Self-Report Information from a Likert Scale

<hr>

A Survey on Making Disciples in Our Church

Directions: Please circle the number on each scale that most represents your personal
  agreement or disagreement with each statement.

1 = strongly disagree	4 = agree
2 = disagree	5 = strongly agree
3 = neither agree nor disagree	

<hr>

My participation in this church over the past six months has helped me

1. to deal with others more kindly and with understanding.

   1   2   3   4   5

2. to ascribe the best of motives to people with whom I disagree rather than the worst
   of motives.

   1   2   3   4   5

3. to forgive hurts and grievances from others rather than to carry them in my heart
   and feelings.

   1   2   3   4   5

4. to increase my regular use of scripture to help me understand my experiences and
   decisions.

   1   2   3   4   5

5. to give more attention and time to others in my life who need my help.

   1   2   3   4   5

6. to increase my financial giving to meet other's needs rather than to meet my own
   satisfaction.

   1   2   3   4   5

<hr>

needed is much deeper and is often referred to as organizational "culture change." In order for us to live into the new and changed mission field, fundamental and familiar norms will have to be changed. Such change is difficult to quickly measure but can be guided by the development of core values for leadership teams to both follow and model for others. Core values are a way for an organization to tell itself what is most important and how decisions are to be shaped in order to accomplish what is most important. The new cultural mission field is now so different and complex that it is not always clear what is the most effective and fruitful thing to do. It is a time in which we need to risk trials and experiments to find our way forward, meaning that we are not yet sure about what works. However, while what to do may not be clear, we can determine how we must do things and what values will guide our steps to signal that we are, at least, headed in the right direction.

In the Arkansas United Methodist Conference, leaders have developed very clear core values which indicate both what values *must* guide their planning and decisions as well as what values *must not* guide their future. For example, one of their four core values is *Establishing the mission field as the primary place for our attention and resources instead of directing most of our attention and resources to the institutional needs of congregations and clergy.*

The "instead of" (a phrase repeated in each of their four core values) is a constant reminder to leaders of how they must now make decisions for the future and how they must break patterns of decision making from the past.

Once core values are identified, it is possible to measure progress in following the paths described by those values. Consider the following work by the Louisiana United Methodist Conference. After describing the preferred future that they believe God calls that conference to live, the leaders of the conference identified the core values that must guide their work as leaders. Their opening statement, "In order to live into our vision for our preferred future, we will live and lead with . . ." is a reminder that, as they search for what they must do for a fruitful future, they do know how they must make their decisions and direct their resources.

What follows is the statement of the Louisiana core values and the Likert scale they developed on the basis of those values. The scale, in modified form in this example, is a tool available to remind leaders of the criteria they are to follow. Importantly, the scale offers brief descriptions of behavior that exemplify each of the values so that leaders can "know it when they see it." Finally, the scale can be used to ask responders to rate their individual or their group performance in being guided by their values.

The Core Values of the Louisiana Conference. In order to live into our vision for our preferred future we will live and lead with . . .

> *Integrity*—We will describe honestly what we see; seek to do the right thing for missional reasons; be forthright and transparent in what we do.
>
> *Accountability*—We will measure our actions and decisions by their connection to the purpose of our mission and we will be accountable to others for this connection to purpose.
>
> *Unrelenting love for all people*—What we do will be for people (in, out & beyond), not for institution, buildings or budgets.
>
> *Courage and risk*—New times call for new actions that will move us ahead even though we may not always be right and will need to learn our next steps from our experiments of risk.
>
> *And holding nothing sacred but the mission*—We will "put all things on the table" for consideration/reconsideration in order to serve the mission.

The modified Likert scale in table 4.4 is based on the above core values.

Table 4.4. A Modified Likert Scale

Criteria	Explanation Rating	1	2	3	4	5
Integrity	I describe honestly what I see.					
Integrity	I seek to do the right thing for missional reasons.					
Integrity	I am forthright and transparent in what I do.					
Accountability	I measure my actions by their connection to the purpose of our mission					
Accountability	I am accountable to others for this connection to purpose.					
Unrelenting love for all people	What I do is for people (in, out and beyond the church), not for institution, buildings or budgets.					
Courage and risk	I engage in new actions (smart risks) to move us ahead even though I may not always be right.					
Courage and risk	I learn next steps from my experiments of risk.					
Holding nothing sacred but the mission	I "put all things on the table" for consideration/reconsideration in order to serve the mission.					
	Total Rating					
0–9	10–18	19–27		28–36		37–45
Unsatisfactory	Improvement Needed	Competent		Highly Effective		Outstanding

Consider how helpful feedback on how well leaders are aligning their discussions and decisions with guiding core values can be when it is not always clear what the right or best decisions must be. With such a tool in place, leaders can take a few minutes at a meeting every several months to complete the scale to ask, "How are we doing?" It is an important tool to keep leaders on track—and to model for others what is important. Perhaps even more helpful, leaders can use the scale at the end of a particularly difficult or contentious time to ask, "How did we do?" Immediate feedback after difficult situations can be invaluable in keeping leaders oriented to their purpose. Examining the collated responses from the tool can even help leaders identify which of the values they best follow and which they most struggle with. We can, indeed, measure our progress in the wilderness.

Logic Models (*10)

The logic model is perhaps the most widely used outcome model of nonprofit organizations. It is a diagrammatic representation that provides a road map for a given program or initiative, showing what the program or initiative is meant to do, with whom, and why. The model generally includes

- target group(s): the individuals, groups or communities to receive the program
- resources to be brought to bear on the targeted problem: personnel, volunteers, physical resources, financial resources, information on target group needs, etc.
- activities: action steps required to achieve program outcomes
- components: a group of conceptually related activities, such as educating, social marketing, etc.[14]

This tool is most useful at the earliest stage of a project because it allows people to grasp at a glance the goals and strategy of a program or an initiative. Making the logic of the project, as well as the resources and activities needed, transparent from the very beginning allows leaders to test the face validity of the plan—does it make sense? From that point, as the leaders begin to get experience with the project, they can review the logic model periodically, testing its effectiveness: Do we see the change happening? Do we have any evidence or stories to confirm what we thought would happen? What have we learned that will shape our next steps?

Consider the example of a church seeking to reach out into their community missionally both to serve the needs of the community and to open their doors to new people. This church has an elementary and middle school immediately across the street. After some homework, church leaders became aware of stresses on families in the community that impact the education of the children. Table 4.5 is an example of a logic model showing how that church could approach their sense of call—that God's vision for their neighborhood is more than is currently experienced—and their conviction that their church could make a difference.

With such a logic model in place, the intent of the program is clear to decision makers in the church as well as to the volunteers who will be asked to support the project. With such a logic model in place, it is easier for church leaders to speak with the principal of the school to identify their intent and seek support and clarification on what boundaries they need to honor between the church and the school. With such a logic model in place, there is a known reason for the pastor to spend a portion of his or her time at the school, a reason for leaders to expend resources to support the project. Most importantly, with such a logic model in place, measures toward the goal can be taken. Leaders can ask for evidence/stories of connections being made, of people seeking help, of agreements of relationship between the school and church, and evidence of a change in the percentage of single-parent families and the percentage of students graduating to the next grade. Multiple measures can be explored to mark progress toward the outcome. The measures taken will guide next steps.

Table 4.5.   Example of a Logic Model

RESOURCES & ACTIVITIES	*If* we invest our pastor's time in working with the school principal; *If* we invest our volunteers and pastor as daily greeters to the school as parents drop off their children; *If* we make our buildings available for school meetings with the community; *If* we provide banners on church property showing our support of the school public to all who go by;
OUTPUTS	*Then* children and parents will be able to identify us as a friendly place of help. *Then* children and parents will be able to identify our pastors and volunteers by name. *Then* children and parents will get familiar with our buildings and will not hesitate to come here. *Then* families will use us for help when they have a need. *Then* we can either meet their need with our own resources and support, or refer them to a place of help.
OUTCOMES	*Then* families in our community will be stabilized and children's education improved as evidenced by • a reduced percentage of single-parent families in the school system; and • an increased percentage of students passing to the next grade level.

If progress is being made, the efforts continue. If little evidence of progress is available, the logic model can be revisited to ask what more must be learned or what additional steps should be tried.

Narrative Results Mapping (*11)

In narrative results mapping we finally enter into an area that has long been problematic in the work of nonprofits where results are not easily quantified. Almost every effort at producing change or helping others can be supported by a story or two of how the project succeeded. So nonprofits often turn to stories to talk about their work. This is anecdotal evidence. It is nonquantifiable evidence of success that is often not verifiable and is most commonly told from the observer's position with no confirmation from others.

Anecdotal evidence, as used by most nonprofits, is commonly a collection of the wrong stories told for the wrong reasons. Most often these stories are told for the purpose of persuasion. The intended impact of the stories is to invite people to believe in the importance of what is being done, or to get people involved in the effort, or to solicit resources for the effort. The intended bottom line of the storytelling is to proclaim, "Look, it's working!" and to suggest, therefore, that it is worthy of the listener's belief, involvement or support. Most commonly, anecdotal evidence is a collection of success stories of change that may, or may not, be the result of the described effort toward the intended outcome. An additional concern is that anecdotal evidence is typically a story about the people involved, not about the process or strategy that is used to try to make a difference.

As such, anecdotal evidence is best used to establish the need for taking up some work to produce change but not for measuring progress or the results of change. For example, my last congregation was located in an urban area with a large number of homeless people. The community was eager to provide programs and resources for homeless women and children but not willing to offer help to homeless men. The work ethic of the people in this city was such that they intuitively believed that if a man was homeless, then it must be his own fault. The unspoken conclusion was that he must have done something wrong or be lazy. No such judgment was placed on women and children because they were more easily seen as dependent and less responsible for their own care. To help clarify the need for helping homeless men, a few volunteers collected stories from men who slept under a nearby bridge. The most powerful story was about a man who had a full-time job and went to work every day despite his living situation. However, he and his wife were separating in an unhappy marriage. He could afford only one apartment with the money he earned, which he gave to his wife and child in order to care for them. He then was homeless. It was a powerful story that broke through the community myth of the lazy wrong-doer and, indeed, convinced the community to initiate help for homeless men. Anecdotal stories can be powerful to help people see a need.

Stories of the lives of these homeless men who then used the program that was subsequently developed were not equally powerful indicators of the success of the program or measures of whether the program was succeeding. Anecdotal stories collected for evidence of effectiveness are routinely collected without any established set of criteria that relates to the program being measured. Ordinarily, they cannot be compiled to support any coherent argument for or against a program. The stories lack causal connection—because it is often very difficult to establish that the difference observed in the story was the outcome of the program being measured. For these reasons, anecdotal evidence is not usually valued in assessing nonprofit work. Funders are suspicious of anecdotal evidence because they know it does not measure effectiveness or project future development toward effectiveness.

Nonetheless, stories are powerful learning tools and, used wisely, can provide exactly the kind of measure needed for the metrics of ministry. Interestingly, Wade Clark Roof spoke of religion and narrative in his 1992 presidential address to the Religion Research Association, a group oriented and skilled in numbers-driven tools of research. In his defense of stories, Roof pointed out that "narrative is motivated by the drive for coherence. Stories have great capacity to bring things together, to sharpen the focus, to help us see things differently."[15] Such coherence is at the root of the strategy of "results mapping," which was developed by Dr. Barry Kibel as an evaluative tool using stories to systematically capture the in-formation found in nonquantifiable anecdotal evidence.[16]

The basic idea of this strategy of measurement is to use the "top few stories" of the organization's work to understand the strengths and weaknesses of a program designed to produce an identified outcome. Kibel assumed that the best stories contained information about what was being done right if the story could be traced from the first interaction between the program and the "client," and each subsequent step in the contact could be reviewed for effectiveness. For example, let's return to our earlier discussion of the church that wanted to change the stability of families in their neighborhood through a relationship with the school across the street. The quantitative metrics they identified for their work were the percentage of single-parent families in the neighborhood and the percentage of students graduating to the next grade level. However, they did not have direct influence over those metrics, and being able to assess the progress of their strategy beyond those quantifiable metrics required a more narrative guide for them to believe they were on the right track.

Using a few top stories of their efforts, the leaders could trace the known specifics of their encounter with neighborhood families from first contact to the point of making a difference—as indicated by a family seeking counseling from the pastor or a family becoming participants in worship and Sunday school. A top story can be reviewed to look at all of the specific connections. How did the volunteers who opened the car doors for the children when their parents dropped them off at school learn a child's name and start a relationship? How did the pastor and volunteers move relationships from learning names to friendly and safe conversations in a brief time? What helped the children and parents connect these friendly helpers they met to the church across the street? How did the meetings between the pastor and principal build collaboration that made the encounter with this family richer? When did this family first enter the church building? Who in the family initiated contact with someone in the church in order to seek help, whom did they contact, what help was requested? . . . and so, the steps of the story could be traced for evidence of progress toward the church's outcome and for information that could improve their efforts.

Results mapping can be an effective tracking device. Note the significant difference in the kind of story that is most helpful. Most often we tell stories about the people we are trying to help. As noted above, these stories may be helpful in proving the need for the work we feel called to. However, the top stories that are important for measuring progress do not focus on the people helped but rather on the process of our strategy for helping. Is there evidence in the story that a strategy or action can or cannot move people in ways we feel called to influence? A review of the specific connections between actions and contacts in the top story can confirm what works well and point to places where we need to rethink and change the approach we are taking.

FROM COUNTS TO MEASURES TO CONVERSATIONS

Counts need to move us to measures, which need to move us to conversations. Peter Drucker wrote,

> The "nonprofit" institution neither supplies goods or services nor controls. Its "product" is neither a pair of shoes nor an effective regulation. Its product is a changed human being. The nonprofit institutions are human-change agents. Their product is a cured patient, a child that learns, a young man or woman grown into a self-respecting adult; a changed human life.[17]

A changed human being is the most important "product" of a congregation or denomination that seeks to offer health, hope and meaning. However, such a product is exceedingly difficult to measure. The dilemma is that without measures of change—if we cannot have conviction that what we do actually moves us toward changing people and changing the world—our churches and denominations are left simply as places busy with their activities, worried about their resources and unsure if all of the activity and worry has any purpose.

We need to faithfully count. We need to move beyond counting to measuring our progress in the wilderness. Small churches and small projects must learn how to use the tools here (and others) in appropriate, informal ways to bend their conversations toward purpose. Large churches and large projects must learn how to use the tools here (and others) in appropriate, formal ways to also bend their conversations toward purpose. Large and small, formally and informally, we must experiment and learn until we know how to talk about what God has called us to do rather than to talk only about what we do when we are busy.

How do we move data to knowledge? How do we move activity to fruitfulness?

FIVE

Cascading Questions

In a linear world, things may exist independently of each other, and when they interact, they do so in simple, predictable ways. In a nonlinear, dynamic world, everything exists only in relationship to everything else, and the interactions among agents in the system lead to complex, unpredictable outcomes. In this world, interactions, or relationships, among its agents are the organizing principle.[1]

In a world of rapid change, leaders too commonly assume that work and life can be neat and tidy, or that it is their task to make work and life neat and tidy. In fact, messiness is the order of the day. Complexity and unpredictability challenge old assumptions of there being a right way to do things. In fact, the *right way* needs to be replaced by the *appropriate way*. This was a lesson taught me years ago in my second church where I served as senior pastor when a member of the church greeted me at the back of the sanctuary weekly with his comment about my sermon, saying, "Gil, that was really appropriate." Week after week Andy would offer the same response to my preaching. Finally, a bit frustrated, I told him that "appropriate" seemed a timid response since I would rather my sermons be engaging, or inspiring or challenging. He simply shook his finger at me and said, no, what I failed to understand is that you can't get better than appropriate. "Appropriate," he said, "means saying what people could hear. If you had said less, it wouldn't help. If you said more, it wouldn't matter." In a nonlinear, dynamic world where everything exists only in relationship to everything else, and the interactions among agents in the system lead to complex, unpredictable outcomes, appropriateness trumps correctness.

At the Texas Methodist Foundation we remain convinced that conversation is the currency of change. In order to live into the change of the world about us as persons of faith, it is important that we have conversations about those things that will lead us faithfully toward God's purpose. In conversation, we learn together what is appropriate as we talk about important things. In a linear time, when change is not swirling about and the steps ahead are known, teaching is an appropriate leadership strategy. When there are clear answers, and the leader knows the answers, then a primary role of leaders is to teach/tell others what to do. But in the current moment when few known answers fit everyone's questions, the learning must be done situation by situation, group by group, congregation by congregation as people talk together, pray together and discover together what is appropriate to do next. *Teaching* by leaders who know the right answers is replaced with *conversations* led by leaders who know the appropriate questions. Where teaching can be generic (one size fits all), conversations must be appropriately specific (i.e., "This is the conversation we must have now because of who we are, where we are and when it is"). "Appropriate" means that the task of leadership is to figure out what conversation is needed in the specific setting and to invite people into that conversation. To talk about less than what is appropriate won't help. To talk about more won't matter.

In his book *The Advantage*, Patrick Lencioni argues convincingly that there are six questions[2] that any healthy organization must be able to answer in order for the people in the organization to have clarity about their purpose and to organize and align themselves around that purpose.

1. *Why do we exist?* (The underlying reason for being, the core purpose.)
2. *How do we behave?* (The set of principles that guide our behaviors and decisions over time, preserving the essence of the organization.)
3. *What do we do?* (The simplest of the six questions—an organization's business definition. If question 1 answers "Why?" then question 3 answers "What?")
4. *How will we succeed?* (Strategy—the collection of intentional decisions an organization makes to thrive.)
5. *What is most important now?* (The need to deal with organization A.D.D. and silos—most organizations have too many top priorities to achieve the level of focus needed to succeed.)
6. *Who must do what?* (At some point leaders need to clarify and unambiguously stipulate what their respective responsibilities are when they go back to work to do their jobs.)

The questions feel linear, all neat and tidy. It would seem that the task of leadership is to start at question 1 and work your way down the list to question 6, answering questions in succession. In reality, the task of leadership is to figure out which question, or questions, must be addressed at any given time. The challenge is not to figure out what the right answer to each question is. As a matter of fact, Lencioni states clearly that "more than getting the right answer, it's often more important to simply have an answer—one that is directionally correct and around which all team members can commit."[3] More appropriately, the issue for leaders is to figure out which question needs attention at any given time to give it needed directional correctness.

It is widely recognized that organizations (congregations and denominations included) live through their narrative—their story about who they are and what they are about. A series of questions such as Lencioni suggests is such a narrative. It is how an organization tells its story, and in the telling it is how the organization brings clarity and alignment to its life. The task of leadership is to care for the story—to assess what part of the story needs conversation and attention at any given time. Because of the fast-changing environment that surrounds all organizations, some questions will need to be periodically revisited simply to be remembered. Other questions, however, will need to be fully reconsidered at times in order to fit the changes surrounding or within the organization. By reviewing, rehearsing and reconsidering the questions, the organization remains, in Lencioni's words, "directionally correct." In the life of congregations and denominations, it is how we remain missionally focused and purposeful. The task of the leader is to continually give the organization (community, congregation, denomination) a better story to tell, a better story to live into. Attention to the appropriate question—the one needing clarification or challenge—is a primary way in which the leader cares for the organization's story and gives it clear purpose.

CASCADING QUESTIONS (*12)

For questions perhaps more specifically designed to be appropriate for congregations and denominations, I suggest that there is a series of cascading questions that enable us to tell our story as communities and institutions of faith. "Cascading" here implies only that the questions are arranged in a sequence. Working with these cascading questions is not a linear process of starting with question 1 and working through to question 9. The task of leaders, as noted above, is to be able to use such a list of cascading questions to be appropriate; to ask, What part of our story is clear and empowering to us now? What part of our story do we need to revisit only to remind ourselves to be bold and faithful? What part of our story do we need to question, examine, challenge and rewrite in order to fit God's purpose now? I suggest that a full list of cascading questions is as follows.

1. Who are we, now? (*The identity question*)
2. Who is our neighbor, now? (*The context question*)
3. What does God call us to do, now? (*The purpose question*)

4. In order to address God's call, what difference do we believe God has called us to make in the next three to five years? (*The outcome question*)
5. What would it look like in three to five years if we are faithful to and fruitful with our call? (*The possibility question*)
6. How will we do it? (*The strategy question*)
7. How will we measure our progress toward fulfilling our call? (*The metrics question*)
8. What have we learned from our experience? (*The learning/evaluation question*)
9. What reshaping or changing do we need to work on because of what we have learned? (*The Ready—Fire—Aim question*)

The story of a congregation, middle judicatory or denomination can be found in these questions, and the answers to these questions form the basis of their story. However, many congregations, middle judicatories and denominations have answers that are only assumptions or generalities. Most threatening to fruitfulness and success are the weak and safe responses to these questions that congregations and denominations have developed over time that will not challenge them beyond the comfort level of their current experience. Leaders must identify false assumptions, vague generalities and weak responses that constrain courage and then invite appropriate conversations that will address the purpose of the organization. It is, in fact, difficult leadership work that requires different tools and assumptions. These nine questions depend upon five different forms of work that leaders need to address, as appropriate, for faithfulness and fruitfulness to God's call.

Descriptive Work

Questions:

1. Who are we, now? (*The identity question*)
2. Who is our neighbor, now? (*The context question*)

It has often been said that one of the first tasks of a good leader is to draw an honest picture of the current reality of an organization or of a people. There are a variety of reasons why we lose track of the reality of the situation in which we find ourselves. One of the primary reasons is familiarity—we are too used to seeing what we have always seen. One simple example is how we (myself included) routinely and regularly think of ourselves as younger than we actually are. Pushed to its limit, what this suggests is that we know more about who we *were* than about who we currently *are*. It takes the occasional strained muscle or the photo taken from an unusual angle to remind us of the difference. Similarly, most of the congregations that I have worked with over a period of decades know much more about who they were than they know about who they are. Familiarity breeds, well, familiarity. It is difficult to see past the picture that we have constructed in our own minds because it is the picture we have constructed. It requires a leader willing and able to take a congregation or middle judicatory back to look again at what we assume we already know about ourselves and our context.

If not familiarity, denial is another reason it is difficult to maintain an honest picture of the current reality. When working with congregations, it is common to find complete and detailed attendance records for worship as long as the attendance is stable or growing. However, it is also fairly common to see congregations stop counting, or stop collating their weekly counts into reports, when attendance begins to shrink. Difficult information is difficult to look at, and a very common, and very human, strategy of dealing with such difficulty is to not look.

So it is that we have congregations with "young couples groups" with an average age in the sixties; middle judicatories still feeling strong despite a loss of 20 percent of their people and 5 percent of their congregations over the past ten years. So it is that congregations continue on without changing their worship style or programming despite living in places where the neighborhood goes through steep changes of ethnic or economic character. Members who move their residence away from the church and drive back into the community on Sunday mornings for worship drive through neighborhoods whose changes they do not see and do not understand. Clergy who have been rostered leaders in their denominational system for a long time in their professional life find it very difficult to accept changed denominational policies or practices despite knowing old policies or practices no longer work. We see what we see because we've always seen it. We do what we do because we've always done it. In working with congregations on strategic planning, I frequently point out how the people who became active in a congregation within the past three years often know more of the reality, positive and negative, of the situation than the members who have been on the governing board and active in leadership over the past thirty years.

Addressing questions of identity and context is simple, descriptive work. Can we describe, again, the people who make up our congregation, our community, our middle judicatory, our denomination? While this can be called "simple" descriptive work, it is actually quite difficult because it is not easy asking a question for which people assume they already know the answer. While I was on staff at the Alban Institute, my colleague Alice Mann and I were responsible for both leading strategic planning in congregations and teaching strategic planning to leaders. As a partial outcome of that work we coauthored a book called *Holy Conversations*,[4] which among other things focuses heavily on discerning a congregation's purpose by beginning with accurate descriptions of the present moment—both inside the congregation and outside in the mission field surrounding the church. The book offers multiple tactics, tools and resources for doing the difficult descriptive work of identity and context. Conversations focused on questions for which people believe they already have the answer are difficult to sustain for a long enough period to allow us to see new things and challenge our assumptions. Yet without a clear and accurate picture of who we are, and where we are, it is impossible to respond to the changed mission field about us.

Discernment Work

   Question:

   3. What does God call us to do, now? (*The purpose question*)

   Discernment work is different from descriptive work. Descriptive work is present tense. It asks for clarity about the reality that currently is. Discernment work moves into the future tense to explore what should be and to explore our role in what is yet to come. In our book *Holy Conversations*, Alice and I suggested that there are three important questions that congregations must be able to answer to discern their purpose and be faithful to God's call. The first two are the questions of identity and context, numbers 1 and 2 above—descriptive work. The third is the question of purpose: What does God call us to do, now? Since writing that book I have learned to ask these questions a bit differently, adding both the comma and the word "now" to the end of each. Who are we, now? Who is our neighbor, now? What does God call us to do, now? The addition of the word "now" is to try to help break through the constraints, familiarity and denial that are discussed above and that keep us locked into knowing only how it was. The comma is just there for emphasis. It invites a verbal and thoughtful pause between the question and the timeframe of the present moment that emphasizes the need to look at the question again even if we think we know the answer.
   Shifting from descriptive to discerning work invites a risk. The work of discernment is not the application of logic, which is why the subtitle to *Holy Conversations* is *Strategic Planning as a Spiritual Practice for Congregations*. The *answers to questions 1 and 2 do not sequentially lead to logical answers to question 3*. This is the work of discernment as described in chapter 3 of this book, which focuses on phronesis and the need to figure things out for ourselves. Phronesis, as described in chapter 3, is practical wis-

dom—it is the conversation, thought, prayer, experience and learning that is applied to the information of descriptive questions 1 and 2 that leads to new insights and stirrings of the heart. Descriptive work can be driven by data and information that leads to conclusions. Discernment is driven by conviction, the intuited awareness that there is something of importance larger than ourselves that God calls us to address.

The Work of Boldness and Courage

Questions:

4. In order to address God's call, what difference do we believe God has called us to make in the next three to five years? (*The outcome question*)
5. What would it look like in three to five years if we are faithful to and fruitful with our call? (*The possibility question*)

Discernment invites boldness and courage. It is a boldness that allows us to presume that if something in the lives of people or in a community is meant to be different, then we can be cocreators with God to bring about that change. But boldness needs specificity and direction that moves us beyond the bravado of tilting against windmills, the false giants that can be attacked safely allowing us to tell tall tales without really making a difference. Ideals are relatively easy to have because they are not specific enough to require engagement. Only when ideals become specific in the current moment and present location are we challenged to gulp and risk making an actual difference. Having an annual community bake sale may allow a congregation to talk about its engagement with the community, but it is a false bravado if the call to that congregation is to actually make some difference in the community. Once the called-for difference is connected to the reality described in questions 1 and 2, courage must kick in to create a boldness that actually seeks change. Boldness is to believe that God calls a congregation to help children in their neighborhood escape poverty, which leads them to provide food to children so that they can engage education with clearer minds that come from satisfied stomachs. Boldness is to understand that wealth can tempt people into thinking that their personal preferences are rights to be exercised over others, an antidote for which the faith community offers spiritual disciplines that can provide a mooring to a fuller life that comes from being in community rather than being over others. Boldness is to know that when countless congregations are struggling to survive without trying to change, denominational resources must be redirected to those congregations, new and old, willing to change to address the changed mission field.

The work of boldness and courage is to risk being specific. In chapter 2 the working definition of an outcome was "The difference that you believe God has called you to make in this next chapter of your life." The difference must be a measureable/describable difference. It has to be something that the leader and the people can clearly aim at in their efforts to be faithful. It is here that this book on metrics seeks to add to the conversation. We need clarity in distinguishing between counting and measuring so that we are sure to be measuring progress toward the difference God claims for us rather than counting what already is. Answering the outcome question (4) and the possibility question (5) means that we commit ourselves to bring about a clear, measureable/describable difference in the lives of people, communities or the world without knowing yet how to do it and without knowing yet if we've got it right.

Naming the difference in question 4 requires the slow, deliberate strategic intuition (see chapter 3) of conversation, prayer, listening and learning—all parts of discernment—until it becomes clear what God asks in a particular circumstance. Our boldness of discernment as leaders is to commit to being certain of moving in the right direction only to also know that in our following that commitment, experience and additional learning will mold the outcome in new ways not easily seen at the beginning. But people need a directional answer to question 4 to know what they are working toward. We all need an aspirational goal that engages our spirits and that gives meaning to our efforts.

Beyond a clear outcome, we also need a picture (question 5, "What would it look like?") of what the world, or our lives, would be like if we should be successful in our goal of producing the difference of our stated outcome. This is the question of possibility, a descriptive statement of what the outcome would look like. It is the picture of children who are freed from poverty by the opportunity of an education that they can pay attention to without the distraction of hunger. It is the picture of people who understand wealth as an invitation to stewardship and responsibility and not as a prerogative of status and personal pleasure. It is the picture of congregations that are energized by possibilities of what is yet to be because of God's presence that goes well beyond their worries about self-care and survival. We respond to possibilities, which produce energy for our spirits. Problems sap energy. The possibility of what a difference would look like if we responded to God's call gives us reason to move ahead.

Implementation Work

Questions:

6. How will we do it? (*The strategy question*)
7. How will we measure our progress toward fulfilling our call? (*The metrics question*)

The implementation work of questions 6 and 7 engages the very familiar part of us which is problem solving and moving to action. It is here that we depend upon our well-exercised logic and our experience of the world that allows us to begin with our if/then assumptions. *If* children in poverty miss meals and do not eat nutritionally, *then* they will have a harder time giving attention and energy to education. But *if* we supplement poverty diets with nutritional food, *then* we increase health and energy that can be directed toward education. And *if* we provide additional healthy food to their diets through backpacks given out at school along with our personal presence and encouragement to work hard at school, *then* they will be both healthier and more motivated. The difference we will make will be better-educated young people who are able to stay in school and are encouraged to continue their education.

We move quickly and easily to strategy, sometimes perhaps too quickly and easily. We put our "ifs" and "thens" together quickly because it is familiar work and they make some logical sense. Often, however, our if/then connections are not tested by experience and reality. We need to pause long enough to ask who else has experience in the area we feel called to work in so that we replace our own naiveté with what others have learned. And we need to identify the tools and the process (chapter 4) by which we will measure the effectiveness of our strategy and our progress toward the difference we believe we are called to make.

Learning Work

Questions:

8. What have we learned from our experience? (*The learning/evaluation question*)
9. What reshaping or changing do we need to work on because of what we have learned? (*The Ready—Fire—Aim question*)

Questions 8 and 9 are the heart of the learning work that allows us to move beyond our initial assumptions to live into the difference we are called to make. This is the learning work of Ready—Fire—Aim (see chapter 3) in which we continually measure and assess our progress toward the difference we are called to make, and continually use our learning from our experience to shape our next steps and correct past missteps.

The quote at the beginning of this chapter stated in part, "In a nonlinear, dynamic world, everything exists only in relationship to everything else, and the interactions among agents in the system lead to complex, unpredictable outcomes." We need paths to follow or else it is difficult to move ahead toward some outcome of difference we discern as our call. But paths are logically constructed and linearly planned, and logic and linear thinking are not, by themselves, up to the task of thriving in a dynamic world of unseen interactions. Questions 8 and 9 keep us in learning mode, which allows us to adjust and readjust our paths toward fruitfulness, depending upon what our immediate past experience can teach us. Constant adjustment and recalibration is a necessity in a fast-changing and interactive environment. When the supersonic Concord passenger jets were still flying, they were equipped with a sensitive navigation system that recalibrated the flight path every several seconds. At super speed, in a complex environment of interactive weather dynamics, too much time without measuring progress and learning from the experience of the immediate environment would send the jet off its intended path and make it miss its destination by a wide margin.

The continued and ongoing learning that we engage in questions 8 and 9 will send us back to earlier questions as appropriate.

APPROPRIATE LEADERSHIP

Cascading questions provide a path for appropriate leadership. It is the task of the leader to know the full set of questions that need to be addressed, and then to know (or intuit) which question or questions need to be reviewed, revised or asked again in a new way in order to continually follow a path toward a God-intended difference. Counting and measuring are tasks along the way, and together they constitute a metrics by which we can measure faithfulness and fruitfulness. But the tools of metrics must always be in the service of purpose. Without a clear conviction of a God-given difference that we are called to make, we cannot reasonably count or measure anything in a meaningful way because they are counts and measures without purpose. We cannot have a clear conviction of a God-given difference that we are called to if we do not have a realistic understanding of who we now are, who our neighbor now is, and what we are now to do about our situation. And so the matrix of questions goes on interactively and interdependently. The tools of metrics are in service to the larger conversation that is shaped by finding the appropriate place in the cascade of questions that drive a life and a community of faithfulness.

SIX

Be Careful What You Measure

In this country the roll of church members is longer than ever before. More than one hundred and fifteen million people are at least paper members of some church or synagogue. This represents an increase of 100 percent although the population has increased by only 31 percent.

The numerical growth should not be overemphasized. We must not be tempted to confuse spiritual power and large numbers. Jumboism, as someone has called it, is an utterly fallacious standard for measuring positive power.[1]

Martin Luther King Jr.'s warning of jumboism was in the midst of the 1960s, a time in which joining organizations, including the church, was at its cultural height. Denominational growth was a cultural trend that had people closely watching church numbers because they were all going up. And yet King warned that numbers were not the standard for measuring the impact of faith. Now in the twenty-first century, we are worried about depletion because our numbers have been dwindling for decades. The warning remains. Our numbers matter deeply. But they are not the standard for measuring the impact of faith. How do we find the balance between measures and purpose? How do we continue to steer our way between our current Scylla and Charybdis to find a way ahead that will not draw us into a false institutionalism driven by too much attention to numbers or draw us into a false complacency from giving numbers too little attention which produces an absence of accountability?

The argument in this book has been pretty straightforward.

1. You get what you pay attention to. If you don't make choices about what is important and measure your progress toward your goals, nothing changes.
2. Counting in the church, by itself, is about resources and activities, not about purpose. We must gather, measure and redirect our resources for the difference we are called to make. But there must be more than attention to resources and activities.

3. Faithfulness and fruitfulness require an intentional purpose that names a difference we feel called to address but is commonly difficult to quantify. Purpose is stated in intentional outcomes, which require measurements instead of counts.
4. Measurements, assessing progress toward outcomes, require new tools and new strategies.
5. We are in a learning mode. Metrics, as a discipline, is new to the church. We are in the process of building new tools, and as with all craftsmen, our learning to use new tools risks injury until the capacity of the tool and our skill as craftsmen are brought together. As we begin, we need to be aware of necessary cautions to new tools.

THREE CAUTIONS WHILE
BUILDING AND USING OUR NEW TOOLS

There are few straight lines in the wilderness. There are times when the way ahead seems quite clear—the pillar of fire appeared in the desert to clearly mark the way the Israelites were to travel. However, there are also times when the way is uncertain, unknown or dangerous—and in those moments, the Israelites "pitched tent" and waited. I can only believe that the Israelites waited actively, which, when steps are uncertain, is what we are called to do. Waiting is a time of preparation. While the Israelites pitched tent, they tested their way forward. Surely they talked with one another, sent scouts to peer over the next horizon, prayed, studied text, rested, rehearsed their purpose and goals, rehearsed what they had already learned, wondered and watched. They reflected on where they were, how far they had come and what the necessary next steps were. The wilderness is a mix of brave movement and also critical reflection.

In every new endeavor there has to be a time of pausing and testing. New insights and ideas must be tested and put into context by experience. One of the basic models of adult learning is referred to as the "adult learning cycle" and reflects this need for pausing and testing which allows for adjusting the way forward (see figure 6.1).

Inherent in this model of learning is the testing by which we try something (Action) and then our reflecting on how it went (Reflection). Is the result what we expected? Were there any surprises? What did we learn? We then connect our reflections to our larger life experience (Connection) and ask, Is that how we understand the world? Have we seen this before? How else have we seen this work? Whom do we know who has had a similar or different experience? Which leads us to a decision of what to do next (Decision), which then leads us to our next step (Action, again).

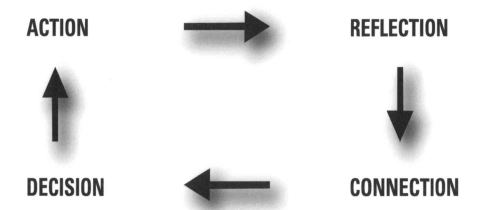

Figure 6.1. Adult Learning Cycle
Source: Patti Simons

Without taking time to "pitch tent," without allowing intentional pauses during which we raise questions and cautions, review, reflect, connect and otherwise test the new ways forward, we can easily over-commit to less-than-helpful paths. When it comes to counting and measuring, there are areas of caution we must test, and we must, based on what we find, be willing to change our direction and learn better ways. At this point there are three basic areas of caution we can be watchful for as we build and use new tools, initiate new practices of using metrics and define new criteria of accountability. The areas of caution that we need to explore are

- short-sightedness
- motivation
- productivity (the appropriateness of measures)

There is a body of literature in each of these areas that can guide our efforts by identifying the pitfalls.

Short-Sightedness

The first caution has to do with short-sightedness—paying too much attention to, and being overly sensitive to, immediate changes so that we lose sight of long-term purpose. In this sense, short-sightedness is looking too near, so that what is still far off goes uncared for. This is the risk of the United Methodist Church overly attending to the metrics of vital congregations by measuring only short-term increases in numbers of people and dollars (and the other counts of resources and activities), while losing sight of the purpose of a vital congregation to change people's lives and transform the world. The risk here is that short-sightedness will capture us in a new institutionalism of organizational measures without leading us to disciple making.

I have been using W. Edwards Deming's basic model of inputs-throughputs-outcomes throughout this book. While working in the U.S. Department of Agriculture, Deming was introduced to the work of Walter Shewhart, who developed a process to bring industrial processes into what was referred to as "statistical control." The real value of statistical control was that it enabled leaders to know where to place their attention, when to act and—importantly—when not to act or overreact.[2] Understanding the idea of statistical control became increasingly important in the 1980s as industry began to pay close attention to quality as an essential element of global-market competition.

By the early 1980s Deming had published his book *Out of Crisis*, in which he identified what he called the "seven deadly diseases" that stood in the way of good management. The first two of these deadly diseases were "lack of constancy of purpose" and "emphasis on short-term profits."[3] He contended strongly that when corporations pursued quarterly dividends and short-term profits (the quick counts) as the basic measures of performance, they were risking their companies by not attending to their purpose. Constancy of purpose, the ability to continuously plan for the improvement of a company's products and services, was more important and life-giving, as opposed to short-term measures that took attention away from the purpose of an organization. Quoting a Japanese colleague, Dr. Yoshi Tsurumi, Deming wrote,

> Part of America's industrial problems is the aim of its corporate managers. Most American executives think they are in the business to make money, rather than products and service . . . The Japanese corporate credo, on the other hand, is that a company should become the world's most efficient provider of whatever product and service it offers. Once it becomes the world leader and continues to offer good products, profits follow.[4]

The caution here, for the United Methodist Church, is that we will need to find our balance between benchmarks and fruitfulness, between the short-term "end-of-quarter" evidence of vitality that comes from counting our resources and activities and our long-term purpose of changing lives and transforming the world.

As I have argued in a number of places, vital congregations are resources—they are nouns. We need vital congregations because they will continue to be the place of community in which disciples are formed. We cannot reasonably think that we will be able to perform our mission of disciple making without healthy, vital congregations. But vital congregations are not the difference we are trying to make. "Constancy of purpose" requires us to always remember that what we are called to produce are disciples of Jesus Christ and a changed world. Vital congregations must always be seen in service to disciple making. In other words, vital congregations are a necessary "proximate outcome" that we must master in our changed mission field in order that we can learn to address our final missional purpose of disciples and a transformed world. At every point we need to rehearse and be directed by our purpose of making disciples and changing the world, while we focus on vital congregations. Our risk is that we will mistake our vital congregation benchmarks and our annual conference dashboards for the purpose of our leadership, and we will react too quickly to the small changes that give evidence to neither fruitfulness nor failure.

As I have argued, it is absolutely essential that we use benchmarks and dashboards to do our counting because without them, we cannot achieve the vital congregations we need for our mission. We cannot sidestep counting simply because it doesn't fully measure what we are finally called to do. Our challenge at the moment, as a denomination, is keeping alive the conversation and the necessary learning about making disciples, while we are redirecting our resources to produce more vital congregations. How do we keep our counts and measures balanced appropriately in our conversations and efforts so that we don't mistake short-term measures as our real purpose?

Connected to Deming's deadly diseases is the mistake of "running a company on visible figures alone."[5] The danger is that we become too sensitive to our benchmarks and dashboards, assuming they measure immediate evidence of progress toward our goals. In our anxiety, we are tempted to become oversensitive to changes in our counts. In part, this is why Deming's method of statistical control was an important tool. Understanding the natural behavior of an industry or an organization enables leaders to know where to pay attention and invest themselves but also when not to act—when not to get too excited and make mistakes. The statistical model introduced "upper and lower limits of control" between which any change or variation produced is simply the nature of the organization and is not the product of efforts made by the leaders. It is a matter of understanding the standard deviation of normal variance.

Consider a real-life example in which the leaders of a church I was asked to work with intentionally set a long-term goal for membership growth in their community, which was experiencing strong demographic growth. Despite their long history of efforts toward a goal of growth, a review of their membership over a twenty-year period showed there had been no real change. Interestingly (and perhaps diabolically!), in the twenty years covered by the data we examined, this congregation received 666 new members. In that same period of time the congregation lost 666 members—for a net change of zero. A part of my work with this congregation was to help them understand their data and to help them address their goal of growth. Naturally, given their continual goal and their lack of any net change after twenty years, the leaders were both frustrated and very anxious about their numbers. One of the first steps in our work was to understand the natural performance of their congregation in a community that was growing (new people coming in) but was also highly mobile as young professionals changed jobs (people going out).

Figure 6.2 is a graph of the membership change in this congregation over the twenty-year period. Note that the highest net annual gain in membership was forty-four members, which can be seen in year 10. The largest loss of members, thirty-four members, can be seen in year 4. The twenty-year history of this church was a continuous oscillation of ups and downs of membership until the total gain matched the total loss.

Particularly important, the leaders talked about their congregation as if it were a roller coaster of "good years" and "bad years." They evaluated their experience and wanted to know what went wrong in bad years and what they did right in good years. They were, in fact, oversensitive and trying too hard to guess what to do next. The reality is that their congregation, in the community in which it was located, was "built" to receive up

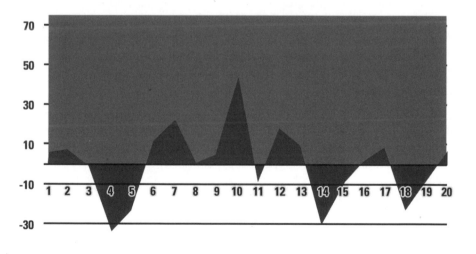

Figure 6.2. Membership Change Graph
Source: Patti Simons

to fifty new members per year and to lose up to fifty members per year, no matter what they did under current conditions. While they worried about good and bad years, what they were actually looking at was the normal variation of an established system that was doing no more than reflecting its environment. This was a primary insight of Deming's focus on statistical control. (Statistically, in the case of this congregation, the mean change was 33.3 people per year; the standard deviation was 5.7; and the upper and lower control limits of variation was 50.6—all meaning that in any given year this congregation could receive fifty new members or lose fifty members simply because of where it was and how it fit into its community.)

The reality was that the congregation went through multiple pastoral changes in the twenty-year period prompted by their concerns about increasing growth, and they sent multiple leaders to multiple continuing education events about church growth in trying to achieve their goal. Their over-attention to counting members pulled their attention away from their purpose as a church in their community. The conversation that was missing was what difference this congregation felt called to make in people's lives and in their community that would want them to engage new people and the mission field around them—and would make people want to engage with them. Their over-sensitivity to annual shifts in membership numbers framed a short-sightedness that made them anxious and over-functioning. What was lost was the balance required by attention to purpose—a longer-term focus on the difference they were called to make.

Churches that count members too closely, and annual conferences that announce progress or set-backs only because there is a slight shift in annual statistics, run the risk of "performance-anxiety" instead of constancy of purpose. Of course, we want to see confirmation of our efforts by watching numbers grow. However, it is not the annual shifts that will confirm our efforts, unless the shifts become a trend over time and exceed the normal limits of the congregational or annual conference systems that we already have. It will still take us a number of years for our denominations to confirm we are on the right path. In the meantime, we will need to carefully and continually rehearse our purpose at each step we take or else our constant counting will hide our need to measure progress toward our disciple-making purpose.

Motivation

Short-sightedness also has a negative effect on motivating people to pursue the purposeful leadership the church needs to address its mission. An inappropriate use of metrics has its negative effect on the passion leaders have for their work. Drawing again from the cautions of Deming,

One of the main effects of evaluation of performance is nourishment of short-term performance.

A [person] must have something to show. [His or her] superior is forced into numerics. It is easy to count. Counts relieve management of the neces-·sity to contrive a measure with meaning. Unfortunately, people that are measured by counting are deprived of pride of workmanship.[6]

Pride of workmanship comes from a sense that one has fulfilled the purpose of one's task. From the contractor who can stand back and look at the studding that he knows will more than adequately support the wall that is needed for a home, to the craftsman who can stand back and look at the wood that she has formed into a table that has as much character as function, to the investment advisor who can sit back knowing that his advice to the client will not just generate income but will also provide security and peace of mind, to the pastor who knows that bringing a person to a commitment of participation or membership is a step toward forming a faith that can transform just living into having life, there is a purpose behind our tasks. To remove the purpose is to diminish the task. The carpenter who doesn't understand that the wall belongs to a home can easily be drawn into using inferior materials or spacing the studs wider than the standard sixteen inches because it can save money and materials. Purpose comes from a sense that there is a "call" to the work we do—a reason beyond the work itself. Without a call, there are only tasks. And a call and a task seek different rewards.

Consider the conversation that is mounting in the church as we try to describe the kind of leadership we believe we need for the future in our changed mission field. We speak of wanting people who are entrepreneurial, agile and missional. An undue reliance on counting resources of people and dollars, without also giving attention to measuring progress toward making disciples and making a difference in our communities and world, can undermine the motivation, passion and creativity of a leader's (clergy and lay) call to the purpose of an entrepreneurial, missional ministry that seeks to find traction in our changed mission field.

Daniel Pink identifies three main drivers that power behavior and have a direct impact on our motivation for doing something. Like versions of software in which later releases are more complex and powerful than earlier versions, he identifies the three drivers as increasingly complex and important.[7]

- *version 1.0*—biological drivers of survival, hunger and thirst
- *version 2.0*—rewards and punishments delivered by the environment (This is based on two simple ideas: rewarding an activity will get you more of it; punishing an activity will get you less of it.)
- *version 3.0*—the intrinsic reward of performance of a meaningful task

We most commonly think of rewards as carrots and sticks—version 2.0. Positive rewards motivate, and so we assume that rewarding congregations and leaders that post good metrics should get us even more good metrics as we seek to change. Lack of good metrics receives the "stick" of not being rewarded, of not receiving attention or of receiving negative attention. So we find annual conferences or synod gatherings bringing pastors and leaders of congregations that have increased their numbers up on the stage at an annual conference session to recognize (and reward) their good work. Or we find denominational leaders holding public gatherings of those church leaders whose congregations have not fulfilled their apportioned missional giving commitment as a negative reward (the "stick" of drawing attention to their lack of covenant commitment). The hope is to reward the behavior we want and to replace the behavior we don't want. In a North American church world in which the biological drivers of 1.0 have largely been cared for, we have turned our attention to the 2.0 drivers of rewards and punishments to shape the response we believe the mission field calls for. To an extent, this is appropriate. If a system gets what it pays attention to, then we need to help our leaders pay attention to the results that we believe will advance our ministry in the mission field, and we need to address the results that don't advance our ministry.

Honoring those who are making progress, as well as calling attention to those who are not fulfilling commitments, in an effort of accountability is vital and important to setting the direction of an organization. The real story of motivation, however, is significantly more complex than that, particularly as it relates to ministry, which is highly connected to the human and community conditions of the unique and immediate setting of the people and mission field involved.

To understand this complexity, Pink provides the distinction between "algorithmic" work and "heuristic" work.

An algorithmic task is one in which you follow a set of established instructions down a single pathway to one conclusion. That is, there is an algorithm for solving it. A heuristic task is the opposite. Precisely because no algorithm exists for it, you have to experiment with possibilities and devise a novel solution.[8]

Given this distinction, it is easy to see that ministry is a heuristic task. There is no single set of behaviors, no standardized set of steps that will produce a person committed to Christ. The path of discipleship is a wandering search through stages of understanding and commitment, not a checklist of activities to be completed.

With heuristic work, with ministry, goals that people set for themselves and that are connected to mastery of their call produce great commitment and effort and are judged to be worth sacrifice—motivation version 3.0. However, goals imposed by others have the dangerous effect of narrowing focus, minimizing creativity, decreasing cooperation and supporting short-term thinking that loses sight of purpose.[9]

Motivation for the heuristic work of ministry (3.0) depends upon staying connected to the meaning of our work—staying connected to the Gospel good news that promises life as more than just living, staying connected to values of community that seek to break boundaries and address suffering. Yes, we must do our counting, and yes, we must recognize those whose "counts" are growing, and yes, we must address those whose "counts" do not contribute to vitality. A system gets what it pays attention to, and we must pay attention.

However, vitality and faithfulness also deeply depend upon continued attention and connection to purpose. Rewards and punishments (2.0), without continued calls to and reminders of purpose (3.0), will not provide either fruitfulness or faithfulness. To move ahead will require continued and increased attention to the other critical steps of heuristic motivation that we are now discovering and using in our changed mission field wilderness:

- annual denominational gatherings that are more focused on worship, spiritual renewal and remembering the purpose of ministry instead of being focused on regulations, resources or decision making
- clergy self-directed peer learning groups as continuing professional development where clergy can remember their call, risk their vulnerability and seek to master their call in the company of other seekers, rather than receive additional information and skills from continuing education "experts" who may or may not be helpful to their setting of ministry
- small group covenant gatherings of laity where relationships, study, and mission help them form as people of faith, rather than reliance only on committee meetings that plan action or classes that teach about a faith that may or may not challenge people to learn a new way of living
- governance meetings (at both the denominational and local church levels) that incorporate study, prayer and reflection into the discernment and decision-making tasks so that actions are not separated from, but rather informed by, our purpose

One of the great cautions of this moment in our church, when we turn to metrics, is the necessity of finding the right balance between drawing attention to and rewarding not only actions and behaviors, but intent and purpose as well. We need to learn how to appropriately reward behaviors by attending to our counts, while we also learn how to appropriately reinforce our passion by underscoring and supporting those things that connect us to our purpose.

Productivity (The Appropriateness of Measures)

And so we come to the third of the cautions—taking care to be sure that our measures are appropriate to, and help to actually produce, the outcome that we are after. Here it would seem that the primary rule is not to be too rigid in our metrics.

In their exploration of practical wisdom, Schwartz and Sharpe use the idea of "bending the rule." In the early days of temple and cathedral construction, "a normal, straight-edged ruler was of little use to the masons who were carving round columns from slabs of stone and needed to measure the circumference of the columns. Unless, you bent the ruler. Which is exactly what the masons did. They fashioned a flexible ruler out of lead, a forerunner to today's tape measure."[10] Practical wisdom requires knowing how to bend the rule to fit the circumstance. Rigid tools do not help. The rigidity of inappropriate or insensitive measures does not help. Observation and experimentation is needed to learn how to bend the rule in the right direction.

Consider how rigid and insensitive measures impact the performance of other professions beyond ministry. We tend to be well aware of this problem in education where effectiveness is measured by standardized testing of students on material determined to be important at each age level. We know that "teaching to the test" overlooks the development of skills and narrows the scope of a child's learning to the subjects and content on which that child will be tested. Evaluating teaching by standardized tests supports memorization as the primary means of learning. Indeed, there was a day in which memorization was an essential tool of the educated person since information was housed in books that resided in libraries, which were often unavailable to people as they worked. However, today information is everywhere and universally accessible to educated people because of the Internet. Memorization, the dominant skill being measured by standardized tests, is a poor substitute for the skills of critical thinking that our children need to learn in order to be able to effectively sift through too much information—that is too available—in order to make good decisions and produce clear outcomes. Standardized tests are necessary tools of measuring. But to actually address our concerns as to whether we are educating our children, we will need to move well beyond rigid measures and bend the rule so that we are more confident that our metrics are actually appropriate to our intended outcomes.

If we look at the profession of law, we can see the same dilemma. A common measure used widely in law offices is the billable hour. A lawyer's productivity is measured by money generated by his or her billable hours, usually accounted for in six-minute segments so a lawyer can reasonably estimate the time spent on a client's questions or problems measured by tenths of each hour. Billing is connected to performance because most law firms recognize and reward the performance of individual lawyers by volume of income brought to the firm. While the billable hour is a clear and honest measure of work done, it can be a questionable measure of fulfilled purpose. If the purpose of a lawyer is to give good counsel to a client, then rigid adherence only to billable hours may be a misdirection of intent. Billable hours, by itself, may encourage a lawyer to poorly serve a client, not by giving poor counsel, but by making counsel overly complex and demanding because it leads to higher revenue. At its worst, billable hours makes the lawyer's supervisor, or the law firm itself, the "client" that the lawyer serves since productivity is measured by income, rather than service of good counsel to the customer.

One can easily go on to medicine where effectiveness is determined by insurance payments to the physician, measured by time spent, diagnoses determined and tests and services provided. The measures are rigid and physicians find themselves shaping their practice to meet the measures. So it is that physicians routinely (and unconsciously) begin to make their diagnosis of a patient's problem within the first fifteen seconds of a visit because payment is based on volume of patients seen in a day. Similarly, because payment is determined by diagnosis and time, physicians so measured will tend to settle on known diagnoses quickly because they fit an insurance provider's diagnostic screen. The physician has little encouragement to spend time listening to the stories of the patient's life where real clues to illness may be hiding, and little encouragement to consider less "diagnosable" causes of a patient's complaint.

In each case, the rigid measures used within a profession direct the professional's work in a way that may not easily bend itself to the profession's purpose. Keep in mind, once again, that this does not suggest that there is no place for such metrics. It does suggest that the wrong or the rigid use of measures that do not fully include the purpose of the practice is not enough.

As argued in this book, limiting our metrics to the rigid counting of resources and activities is insufficient and, by itself, may be misdirecting. Our categories of counts in the church are insensitive. We count members at a time when people are not looking for membership in organizations. We count professions of faith in a way that can encourage congregations to think of this step as a final mark of discipleship rather than an entry point. We need to include counting, but we need to move beyond the limits of only counting in order to experiment with measures that will guide us to the real changes that we believe we are called to make.

This chapter began with a 1963 quote from Martin Luther King Jr. that warned of over-attention to numbers and size. From the last half of the twentieth century into the beginning of the twenty-first century, attention to size has dominated. Some claimed, at an earlier time, that our numbers indicated the importance of the church; some now point to the numbers as evidence of the irrelevance of the church. Some are hopeful; some are critical. Whatever the size of the church, its purpose is not diminished. In the same sermon, King went on to say, "Many continue to knock at the door of the church at midnight, even after the church has so bitterly disappointed them, because they know that the bread of life is there."[11] First, and above all, if we are true to our purpose as the holders of the bread of life, and if we learn to offer this bread to the new cultural mission field around us, then constancy of purpose will care for our counts and measures. Counting and measuring are simply tools we use to hold ourselves accountable to the purpose of God's dreams for us and for our world.

Resources

The resources in this section are intended for use by leaders in a variety of settings. Recognizing that leaders will want to reproduce these materials for use in larger-group settings, Rowman & Littlefield has also made these resources available as a PDF formatted for easy and clear printing on 8 ½" × 11" paper. These resources may be printed and reproduced in limited quantities for private use without obtaining written permission. To acquire a copy of the PDF version of these resources, please email **resourcematerial@rowman.com** with your request, providing both the title and author of the book, *Doing the Math of Mission* by Gil Rendle, along with proof of purchase.

Due to copyright protection issues, any part of this book beyond this resource section may not be reproduced in any form without written permission from Rowman & Littlefield. For more information on reproducing resources that do not appear on the website, or other materials in *Doing the Math of Mission*, go to **https://rowman.com/Page/RightsPermissions**.

CONTENTS

Counting and Measuring:
A Systems Approach
(Resource #1)

Counting is giving attention to numbers. When counting, the question to be answered is "how many?" Conversations about "how many" are most frequently conversations about resources. Conversations about resources, in a time of limited resources, are commonly conversations about scarcity—"do we have enough?" or, "how can we get more?"

Measuring is giving attention to change. When measuring, the question is not about "how many?" but rather about "how far?" Conversations about "how far" are frequently about the change that can be measured over time as in, "how far have we come, over the past year, toward our goal?"

Notables:

1. At the heart of the church's struggle to be fruitful is the common non-profit dilemma: nonprofits routinely do not know what difference they are trying to make. In other words, nonprofits (of which churches and conferences are examples) do not know what outcome they are trying to produce.
2. Congregations and denominations commonly confuse their ideal (their mission statement) with their outcome (what they must make different as a next step toward their ideal). Ideals must be translated

INPUT	THROUGHPUT	OUTPUT / OUTCOME
Resources	**Activities**	The difference or change
(Nouns)	(Verbs)	to be accomplished

[- - - - - - - - COUNTING - - - - - - - -]   [- - - MEASURING - - -]

The Deming Systems Model

COUNTING	MEASURING
Focus is on resources and activities—What currently is	Focus is on outcomes—Intended differences of what is not yet
Answers the questions of how many, how often, and how much	Answers the question of how far we have moved toward our intended difference
Indicator of strength, health, potential	Indicator of movement toward the goal
Related to vitality	Related to purpose
Axiomatic and belonging to every congregation/conference	Unique and specific to each congregation/conference

into outcomes by asking "what must we now make different in order to move toward our ideal?"

3. The local congregation or conference must be able to describe the intended change that they believe they are called to produce, so they can talk about whether or not they are moving toward their goal.

4. The word "describe" is used intentionally in reference to outcomes because in nonprofit organizations, outcomes are commonly difficult to reduce to quantifiables. A clear difference is intended and needed, but is not often easily quantifiable.

5. Without a description there is no way for leaders to have a conversation about whether they are making progress toward their outcome.

6. Because resources and activities are more easily counted, the temptation of non-profits, when they are not clear about their outcomes, is to count their inputs and activities.

7. Change is a fundamental bottom line of faith, and therefore about faith communities. People who have encountered Christ should have behavior that has been changed from those who have not encountered Christ. Christian congregations should be seeking to change the corner of the kingdom of God they have been given (their mission field) because of their faith.

8. There is a need for both counting and measuring. In all complex tasks of leadership, multiple tools are needed. However, like all tools, the right tool must be chosen for the job at hand.

Outcome: A Working Definition
(Resource #2)

"For the church, an outcome is (1) the difference that (2) you believe God has called you to make (3) in this next chapter of your life."

An outcome is:

1. **the measurable/describable difference:** The fundamental and obvious proposition of the Christian faith is that because Christ is in our lives, something should be different. We should be different. Our relationships with others should be different. What we give ourselves to should create a difference. We are not here to preserve and protect, but to challenge and change.
2. **you believe God has called you to make,** i.e., the product of the purpose God has given you—what is to be different—is not about our preferences but about God's purpose. The outcome of a congregation is not about what we can think of to do next but about what God calls us to make different. A faithful outcome of healthy ministry requires more discernment of God's will than decision-making about our own future.
3. **in this next chapter of your life,** i.e., to be accomplished in a clearly defined, and relatively brief, period of time: An outcome is not for all time but is the necessary next step of development toward the larger dream that God has but which we cannot yet fulfill. Outcomes are time limited. They are about what we need to learn how to do, how to live, next.

Learning to Talk About Outcomes Instead of Process

(Resource #3)

From: Outcome Frameworks: An Overview for Practitioners

—Penna and Phillips

QUESTIONS OF *PROCESS* LEAD TO ANSWERS OF ACTIVITIES AND RESOURCES:

Process-Focused Interview
Q.　What does your organization do?
A.　We provide services to low-income residents of our community.
Q.　What kinds of services?
A.　We provide group and individual family counseling.
Q.　How many people do you serve?
A.　Last year we provided 500 counseling hours to 125 families.

QUESTIONS OF *OUTCOME* NAME / DESCRIBE THE DIFFERENCE TO BE MADE:

Outcome-Focused Interview
Q.   What is your organization hoping to accomplish? A.   We are working to improve the parenting skills of abusive families. Q.   What kind of skills improvements are you working toward? A.   Reductions in use of corporeal punishment and increases in uses of positive reinforcers of good behavior, among others. Q.   For the coming year, what level of results would make the year a success? A.   For the coming year, we are working to improve parenting behavior in 200 families (as measured by the use of corporeal punishment or the use of reinforcement of good behavior).

PROCESS AND OUTCOME QUESTIONS VIEWED SIDE-BY-SIDE

Process-Oriented Question	Outcome-Oriented Question
What housing services do you offer?	What community results do you hope to accomplish through your housing services?
What is it that your agency does?	What is your organization striving to achieve?
What service needs does your agency meet?	What changes in conditions or behavior are you attempting to effect in the people you serve?
What services must we offer to prevent our community from further deterioration?	What would be the ideal mix of people and businesses to make our community more desirable?

Process-Oriented Question	Outcome-Oriented Question
How can we overcome the learning challenges students bring with them to school?	What skill sets and knowledge must our children possess to be successful?
What public information strategies do you use?	What changes in attitude are you attempting to effect and with what specific groups?

It may well be that in order to learn how to work with outcomes, we will need to first learn how to ask questions that prompt outcome responses. As noted above, it matters what question one asks because within the question is a clue to the answer. Consider the old story of the priest who went to his superior to ask if he could smoke while he prayed, only to be told "no." Another priest went to the same supervising father to ask if he could pray while he smoked, to which the answer was, "Yes, of course, my son." It matters how we ask the question.

The Grameen Bank Ten Indicators
(Resource #4)

A Nonprofit Example of *Clear Outcomes*:
Muhammed Yunus, founder of Grameen Bank, received the Nobel prize for his pioneering work in microlending to the very poor in Bangladesh. Like other lending institutions, Grameen Bank uses obvious process metrics of numbers of borrowers, size of loans, rate of repayment, and other profitability indicators. These, however, are just the measures of inputs and throughputs, the resources used and the activities pursued in making loans. The real purpose of Yunus's work is to change the socioeconomic situation of its members and to move people out of poverty. One could simply offer loans and hope that it would help people out of poverty. But Grameen Bank did the hard work to precisely define "out of poverty" by developing its Ten Indicators.

The Grameen Bank Ten indicators:
A member is considered to have moved out of poverty if her family fulfills the following criteria:

1. *The family lives in a house worth at least Tk.25,000 (about $350) or a house with a tin roof, and each member of the family is able to sleep on a bed instead of on the floor.*
2. *Family members drink pure water out of tube-wells, boiled water or water purified by using alum, arsenic-free purifying tablets or pitcher filters.*
3. *All children in the family over six years of age are going to school or finished primary school.*
4. *Minimum weekly loan installment of the borrower is Tk.200 (approx. $2.81) or more.*
5. *Family uses sanitary latrine.*
6. *Family members have adequate clothing for everyday use, warm clothing for winter, such as shawls, sweaters, blankets, etc. and mosquito-nets to protect themselves from mosquitoes.*
7. *Family has sources of additional income, such as vegetable garden, fruit-bearing trees, etc., so that they are able to fall back on these sources of income when they need additional money.*

8. *The borrower maintains an average balance of Tk. 5,000 ($70) in her savings account.*
9. *Family experiences no difficulty in having three square meals a day throughout the year, i.e., no member of the family goes hungry any time of the year.*
10. *Family can take care of (its) health. If any member of the family falls ill, family can afford to take all necessary steps to seek adequate health care.*

Three Essential Types of Leadership Conversations

(Resource #5)

In the years that North American denominations have been experiencing shrinking membership and resources we have learned quite a bit about leadership. Where we once defined leadership in terms of the decisions a leader made on behalf of others, the most recent focus has been on the conversations that leaders invite others into. Conversation is the currency of change. What we invite people to talk about, to think about, to pray about, determines the path that we will follow into the future. Leaders have the power of agenda—they have the responsibility of determining what a congregation or denomination will focus on by giving time and attention to a conversation. We are currently in a moment in which there are three essential types of conversations to which leaders can invite others.

Maintenance conversations have a primary focus on preserving who we were and following the rules already set. However, maintaining too much attention on the norms, policies, rules and traditions that we have accrued over time can be stultifying to a people who now need to gather energy and courage to enter into a changed cultural mission field where old ways have become ineffective. Maintenance conversations have their place, but easily undermine the very mission (and changes) to which God now calls us.

Preferential conversations focus on satisfying the people who are already in our congregations, or focus on attracting the people that we wish were in our congregations. Preferential conversations also have an appropriate place in our work. In any mission field, the carriers of the Good News have to first learn the language and the ways of the indigenous people. We need to understand the preferences of the people we are called to serve. Preferential conversations, however, easily slip into judgments about the right way and wrong way to go about things. Too often focusing only on our preferences for the way in which something is done too easily trumps the importance of doing it. At its most limited, preferential conversations devolve into the search for ways to keep people happy and unchanged instead of being challenged and reshaped by the demands of the Gospel.

Missional conversations focus on purpose and on the possibility of the future. The origin of the word "mission" is mid-sixteenth century denoting the sending of the Holy Spirit into the world, from the Latin *missio* or *mittere* meaning "send." To send is to talk about what is not yet, what is possible with the sending of the Holy Spirit. It is here that clarity of purpose and outcomes is most important in order to participate with the Holy Spirit to address that which is not yet accomplished. Discernment about what God dreams for us, and for which God sends his Spirit, requires a specificity about what is yet to be if we are to be the helping hands to make it so.

QUESTION: WHAT CONVERSATIONS ARE YOU HAVING?

Congregational Vitality Index
(Resource #6)

The **Vitality Index** consists of the benchmarks for a vital congregation developed in response to the Call to Action research in the United Methodist denomination.

(All percents refer to U.S. United Methodist Congregations)

GROWTH

- On average, U.S. highly vital congregations increase worship attendance by 4 percent over five years. The average worship attendance change for all U.S. churches is −7 percent.
- On average, U.S. highly vital congregations increase the number of professions of faith by 82 percent over five years. The average change in the number of professions of faith for all U.S. churches is −11 percent.

INVOLVEMENT

- On average, U.S. highly vital congregations have 106 percent of their worship attendance involved in a small group or some ongoing study opportunity. This number may seem inaccurate, but it exceeds 100 percent because the average worship attendance does not include some people who go to small groups like children in Sunday School or youth in youth group. The average for all U.S. churches is 5 percent.
- On average, U.S. highly vital congregations have 9 percent of their worship attendance who are young adults involved in study groups that include Bible study, Sunday School, and other groups for learning. The average for all U.S. churches is 5 percent.
- On average, U.S. highly vital congregations have 56 percent of their total professing members in average worship attendance. The average for all U.S. churches is 51 percent.

ENGAGED

- On average, U.S. highly vital congregations have 20 percent of their worship attendance engaged in a volunteer in mission ministry. The average for the U.S. is 8 percent.
- On average, U.S. highly vital congregations have 6 percent of their worship attendance that join by profession of faith or are restored in a given year. This does not include confirmands. The average for U.S. churches is 2 percent.

GIVING

- U.S. highly vital congregations give 100 percent of their apportionments for the most current year.
- On average, U.S. highly vital congregations grow mission giving by 12 percent over five years. The average for all U.S. churches is −15 percent.
- On average, U.S. highly vital congregations grow non-capital spending by 22 percent over five years. The average for all U.S. churches is 2 percent over five years.

The Shape of an On-Going Outcome Conversation

(Resource #7)

Getting to our outcome is commonly not a straight path of making a decision and then acting. Rather, getting to our outcome is a continual process set by boldness and a belief in God's difference in our world followed by on-going conversation and discernment marked by action, measurements, and learning. The nature or shape of an on-going outcome conversation may be thought of as follows:

1. Question God's purpose for your church or conference for the next three to five years.
2. Dream big. Be bold about what you can make different because it moves you closer to fruitfulness in your purpose.
3. Commit to making a difference in the lives of people or your community, and name the difference (outcome), describing it as deeply as you can.
4. See how/ask what other churches or conferences know about achieving your outcome. Search the literature. Use your own experience to learn next steps.
5. Work hard.
6. Measure results. Constantly track "how far" you are getting to your outcome.
7. Repeat again, starting with step #3.

Apgar Scores:
A Tool of Measurement
(Resource # 8)

An **APGAR SCORE** is a simple self-report instrument asking people "do you see it or not?" It asks participants for an immediate opinion of whether they did or did not observe a desired behavior in a group's work. At the conclusion of some work, participants are asked to score the tool, as instructed in the directions, based on their own experience and perspective. No further definition is given to the desired behaviors. The responses of the individual participants may then be collated to offer a group's self-assessment of their work and to suggest places where they may need to give further attention.

The example below comes from a governing board of a local congregation that was wrestling with their decisions about whether resources should be directed toward church management and maintenance (updating computers, purchasing storm windows) or the development of people's spiritual lives (providing discipleship training or mission trip opportunities). They found themselves in the biblical story of Mary and Martha, Luke 10. Martha and her concern for doing the dishes was the voice of management and maintenance. Mary and her desire to sit at the feet of Jesus was the voice of the development of people's spiritual lives. They used this tool to test their balance of the two voices in their governing board meetings.

Suggestions for developing an APGAR SCORE instrument:

1. Be sure to frame the statements in terms of observable behaviors, not on attitudes or feelings.
2. State the observable behavior in a positive statement.
3. Direct participants to use a simple 3-stage Yes/No scale: 0= No, not at all; 1= Yes, at times; 2= Yes, we did).

Suggestions for using an APGAR SCORE instrument:

1. Invite participants to score the instrument individually based on their own personal experience of the situation.

Honoring "Martha" (church management and maintenance) and "Mary" (the development of people's spiritual lives) Rate each of the following statements by placing after each statement a number from 0 ("Not at all.") to 2 ("Yes, we did.") based on your experience at this meeting.	Nos. 0 to 2
1. We honored both Martha and Mary by giving attention to each in our meeting.	No. _____
2. We collaborated in our work rather than competed for attention and resources.	No. _____
3. We treated one another with respect and cared for our relationships as we worked.	No. _____
4. We listened to each other, seeking to understand.	No. _____
5. Our work focused on the future of our ministry rather than on the past.	No. _____
TOTAL:	No. _____

2. Invite participants to score the instrument anonymously. The value of the responses is in the aggregate assessment by the group, not in the individual responses. Inviting anonymity also encourages truth-telling since individual scores will not be revealed.
3. Collate the responses and report the collated summary to the full group.
4. Invite the group to reflect on the scores together. Celebrate the group's ability to behave as desired if the data corroborates success. Ask for group reflections on why some, or all, behaviors are difficult to follow if the data corroborates difficulty. Ask for group reflections on why some behaviors are more difficult to follow if the data corroborates differences.
5. Invite individuals to reflect on the extent to which their own individual scores did, or did not, align with the group's collated score. Reflections on individual responses may be invited for public sharing, but are not to be required.

6. Keep the summary collated responses in a file for later comparison with additional uses of the same APGAR SCORE instrument with the same group of leaders. Repeated use of the same instrument allows for measures of increased proficiency to behave as desired or allow for identification of which behaviors are routinely difficult.

Suggestions for times in which to use an APGAR SCORE instrument:

1. In the last 15 minutes of every meeting of the leadership group following the time in which the desired behaviors were identified. Continue at the end of each meeting for 3 to 5 meetings.
2. Periodically, once a quarter, for a year to track improvements or difficulties with the behaviors.
3. Immediately following a contentious meeting or conversation.

Likert Scales:
A Tool of Measurement
(Resource #9)

Likert scales are self-report instruments named after American educator and organizational psychologist Rensis Likert. A Likert scale is a "psychometric" instrument. It measures knowledge, abilities, attitudes or personality traits by offering scaling responses in survey style. It provides a means for capturing variation. We have all used these scales in a variety of settings, and the basic form below should look familiar:

To what extent have I/we (insert the behavior to be observed and measured):

1	2	3	4	5

1 = not at all
2 = not much
3 = about the same
4 = some
5 = a good deal

The Likert scale is simply a statement, which the respondent is asked to evaluate according to any kind of subjective or objective criteria determined by the respondent. As such, it is a "self-report" instrument—it reports on our own perceptions and judgments. It is an invaluable tool of direct feedback, making our perceptions and judgments transparent to us in a way that allows for conversation and decision-making. Likert scales are particularly helpful with variables that are not easily quantifiable.

Likert scales are easily adaptable. Please see chapter 4, "Counts, Measures and Conversations: Using New Tools for Fruitfulness," for examples:

- A scale for use as a survey of people in a congregation which measures responses in comparison to research on healthy congregations.

- A scale for use in a congregation to measure change within the individual spiritual lives of participants because of their participation in the congregation (also on the next page of this handout).
- A scale for measuring how far a middle judicatory leadership group is progressing in following its own core values in working together and making decisions.

A Survey on Making Disciples in Our Church

Directions: Please circle the number on each scale that most represents your personal agreement or disagreement with each statement.

1 = strongly disagree	4 = agree
2 = disagree	5 = strongly agree
3 = neither agree nor disagree	

My participation in this church over the past six months has helped me:

1. to deal with others more kindly and with understanding.

   1   2   3   4   5

2. to ascribe the best of motives to people with whom I disagree rather than the worst of motives.

   1   2   3   4   5

3. to forgive hurts and grievances from others rather than to carry them in my heart and feelings.

   1   2   3   4   5

4. to increase my regular use of scripture to help me understand my experiences and decisions.

   1   2   3   4   5

5. to give more attention and time to others in my life who need my help.

   1   2   3   4   5

6. to increase my financial giving to meet other's needs rather than to meet my own satisfaction.

   1   2   3   4   5

Suggestions for developing a Likert Scale instrument:

1. Identify the critical behaviors or other evidence that will indicate movement toward the specific outcome identified by leaders in their planning.

2. Be sure to frame the statements in terms of observable behaviors or evidence, not on attitudes or feelings.
3. State the observable behavior or evidence in a positive statement.
4. Direct participants to circle the number of the scale of each question based on their personal agreement with the statement.

Suggestions for using a Likert Scale instrument:

1. Invite participants to score the instrument individually based on their own personal experience of the situation.
2. Invite participants to score the instrument anonymously. The value of the instrument is in the aggregate assessment by the group, not in the individual responses. Inviting anonymity also encourages truth-telling since individual scores will not be revealed.
3. Collate the responses.
4. Invite leaders to reflect on the scores together. Celebrate movement toward the outcome if the data corroborates success. Use the collated responses for additional learning that can further direct or re-direct the strategy toward outcomes as appropriate.
5. Share the collated response with the full group/congregation as an opportunity to remind people what is important behavior and to invite individual reflection about their own personal behavior.
6. Keep the summary collated responses in a file for later comparison with additional uses of the same Likert scale instrument with the same group of participants or leaders. Repeated use of the same instrument allows for measures of increased proficiency to behave as desired or allow for identification of which behaviors are routinely difficult.

Suggestions for times in which to use a Likert scale instrument:

1. When used with leadership groups focused on their own leadership outcomes: In the last 15 minutes of every meeting following the time in which the desired behaviors were identified. Continue at the end of each meeting for 3 to 5 meetings.
2. When used with leadership groups focused on their own leadership outcomes: Immediately following a contentious meeting.
3. When used with large groups or congregational participants: Once every 6 to 12 months to track progress toward the goals set by leaders in their outcomes.

Logic Models:
A Tool of Measurement
(Resource #10)

The logic model is perhaps the most widely used outcome model of non-profit organizations. It is a diagrammatic representation that provides a road map for a given program or initiative, showing what the program or initiative is meant to do, with whom, and why. The model generally includes:

- Target group(s): the individuals, groups or communities to receive the program.
- Resources to be brought to bear on the targeted problem: personnel, volunteers, physical resources, financial resources, information on target group needs, etc.
- Activities: action steps required to achieve program outcomes
- Components: group of conceptually related activities, such as educating, social marketing, etc.

This tool is most useful at the earliest stage of a project because it allows people to grasp at a glance the goals and strategy of a program or an initiative. Below is an example of a logic model from a congregation seeking to make changes in their community by working with a public school across the street from the church.

Making the logic of the project, as well as the resources and activities needed, transparent from the very beginning allows leaders to test the face validity of the plan—does it make sense? From that point, as the leaders begin to get experience with the project they can review the logic model periodically, testing its effectiveness: Do we see the change happening? Do we have any evidence or stories to confirm what we thought would happen? What have we learned that will shape our next steps?

Suggestions for developing a logic model:

1. Be as clear as possible about:
   a. Target group(s): the individuals, groups or communities to receive the program

RESOURCES & ACTIVITIES	*If* we invest our pastor's time in working with the school principal; *If* we invest our volunteers and pastor as daily greeters to the school as parents drop off their children; *If* we make our buildings available for school meetings with the community; *If* we provide banners on church property showing our support of the school public to all who go by;
OUTPUTS	*Then* children and parents will be able to identify us as a friendly place of help. *Then* children and parents will be able to identify our pastors and volunteers by name. *Then* children and parents will get familiar with our buildings and will not hesitate to come here.
OUTPUTS	*Then* families will use us for help when they have a need. *Then* we can either meet their need with our own resources and support, or refer them to a place of help.
OUTCOMES	*Then* families in our community will be stabilized and children's education improved as evidenced by • a reduced percentage of single-parent families in the school system; and • an increased percentage of students passing to the next grade level.

    b. Resources to be brought to bear on the targeted problem: personnel, volunteers, physical resources, financial resources, information on target group needs, etc.

    c. Activities: action steps required to achieve program outcomes.

    d. Components: group of conceptually related activities, such as educating, social marketing, etc.

2. Separate the outputs (the proximate changes you seek) that will lead you to outcomes (the end change that you seek, that may be beyond your immediate control).

Suggestions for using a logic model:

1. Develop the logic model as an exercise of planning so that you are clear about what activities and resources you will use to achieve the desired outcome.
2. Return to the logic model periodically and consistently to seek evidence that you are moving toward your outcome, and to identify where resources and activities are not producing the change desired.
3. Use the logic model to continually change and adapt your work based on what you are learning.
4. Adapt the logic model itself to reflect the changes that you tried that do produce the outcome desired.

Narrative Results Mapping:
A Tool of Measurement
(Resource #11)

The basic idea of this strategy of measurement is to use the "top few stories" of the organization's work to understand the strengths and weaknesses of a program designed to produce an identified outcome. The best stories contained information about what is being done right if the story could be traced from the first interaction between the program and the "client," and each subsequent step in the contact could be reviewed for effectiveness. Results mapping can be an effective tracking device. Consider the significant difference in the kind of story that is most helpful. Most often we tell stories about the people we are trying to help. These stories may be helpful in proving the need for the work we feel called to. However, the "top stories" that are important for measuring progress do not focus on the people helped, but rather on the process of our strategy for helping. Is there evidence in the story that a strategy or action can or cannot move people in ways we feel called to influence? Can we confirm, or must we adapt, the way we are moving toward our outcome?

For example, consider the discussion in chapter 4, "Counts, Measures and Conversations," of the church that wanted to change the stability of families in their neighborhood through a relationship with the school across the street. The quantitative metrics they identified for their work were the percentage of single-parent families in the neighborhood and the percentage of students graduating to the next grade level. However, they did not have direct influence over those metrics and being able to assess the progress of their strategy beyond those quantifiable metrics required a more narrative guide for them to believe they were on the right track.

Using a few "top stories" of their efforts, the leaders could trace the known specifics of their encounter with neighborhood families from first contact to the point of making a difference—as indicated by a family seeking counseling from the pastor or a family becoming participants in worship and Sunday school. A "top story" can be reviewed to look at all of the specific connections. How did the volunteers who opened the car doors for the children when their parents dropped them off at school learn the child's name and start the relationship? How did the pastor and volunteers move relationships from learning names to friendly and safe conversations in a brief time? What helped the children and parents connect these friendly helpers they met to the church across the street? How did the meetings between the pastor and principal build collaboration that made the encounter with this family richer? When did this family first enter the church building? Who in the family initiated contact with someone in the church in order to seek help, who did they contact, what help was requested? . . . and so, the steps of the story could be traced for evidence of progress toward the church's outcome and for information that could improve their efforts.

Cascading Questions
(Resource #12)

The series of cascading questions that follows enable us to tell our story as communities and institutions of faith. "Cascading" here implies only that the questions are arranged in a sequence. Working with the cascading questions is not a linear process of starting with #1 and working through #9. The task of leaders is to be able to use such a list of cascading questions to be appropriate; to ask: what part of our story is clear and empowering to us now?; what part of our story do we need to revisit only to remind ourselves to be bold and faithful?; what part of our story do we need to question, examine, challenge and rewrite in order to fit God's purpose now? To complete answers to these questions requires different forms of leadership work.

DESCRIPTIVE WORK

1. Who are we, now? *(The identity question)*
2. Who is our neighbor, now? *(The context question)*

DISCERNMENT WORK

3. What does God call us to do, now? *(The purpose question)*

THE WORK OF BOLDNESS AND COURAGE

4. In order to address God's call, what difference do we believe God has called us to make in the next 3 to 5 years? *(The outcome question)*
5. What would it look like in 3 to 5 years if we are faithful and fruitful with our call? *(The possibility question)*

IMPLEMENTATION WORK

6. How will we do it? *(The strategy question)*
7. How will we measure our progress toward fulfilling our call? *(The metrics question)*

LEARNING WORK

8. What have we learned from our experience? *(The learning/evaluation question)*
9. What reshaping or changing do we need to work on because of what we have learned? *(The Ready—Fire—Aim question)*

The story of a congregation, middle judicatory or denomination can be found in these questions, and the answers to these questions form the basis of their story.

Notes

INTRODUCTION

1. A "dashboard" is a certain set of measures that is used as indicative of the overall health or operation of a system. As with automobiles, which have become increasingly complex and computer driven, the number of measures of performance available is well beyond the need or comprehension of the driver who simply wants to know if the car is running well or not. So drivers learn to attend to the dashboard—the most essential measures that show up, quite obviously, on the dashboard. Drivers need to know if there is sufficient gas, sufficient oil, if the engine is overheating and if there is a maintenance or equipment issue of sufficient importance to turn on the little light. If the dashboard indicates the right levels and does not light up the wrong icons, it means all is well and the travel can continue. But negative measures posted or warnings flashing means action must be taken.

2. An edge organization is one that lives on the edge of a mother institution, movement or effort. In this case, TMF is clearly "of" the United Methodist Church but is not "in" the United Methodist Church, which is to say that it is neither directed by nor constrained by the denomination. The edge is a particularly fertile place from which to pursue an organization's purpose.

CHAPTER 1

1. Eugene Peterson, *The Message: The Bible in Contemporary Language* (Colorado Springs: NavPress Publishing Group, 2002), 1769.

2. Beverly Roberts Garenta and David Peterson, eds., *The New Interpreter's Bible One-Volume Commentary* (Nashville, TN: Abingdon, 2010), 697.

3. Christopher Beeley, *Leading God's People: Wisdom from the Early Church for Today* (Grand Rapids, MI: Eerdman's, 2012), 54.

4. For a fuller discussion of Deming's model and its application to the changed paradigm we now face in the mainline church, please see Gil Rendle, *Back to Zero: The Search to Rediscover the Methodist Movement* (Nashville, TN: Abingdon, 2011), 37–46.

5. Jim Collins, "Good to Great and the Social Sectors," www.jimcollins.com, 2005.

6. Reggie McNeil, *Missional Renaissance: Changing the Scorecard for the Church* (San Francisco: Jossey-Bass, 2009).

CHAPTER 2

1. William Sloane Coffin, *Credo* (Louisville, KY: Westminster John Knox Press, 2004), 140–41.

2. Robert Penna and William Phillips, *Outcome Frameworks: An Overview for Practitioners* (Delmar, NY: Rensselaerville Institute, 2004), 6.

3. Ibid., 7f.

4. Jim Collins, "Good to Great and the Social Sectors," www.jimcollins.com, 2005.

5. Peter Drucker, *Managing the Non-Profit Organization: Principles and Practices* (New York: Harper Business, 1990), xiv.

6. Collins, "Good to Great."

7. Andras Szanto, "Art Basel," *Miami Beach Daily*, December 1, 2011. This article was passed on by my friend Gary Keene, a colleague who understands that the church has much to learn by looking at other organizations, industries and professions.

8. Steve Rothschild, *The Non Nonprofit: For-Profit thinking for Nonprofit Success* (San Francisco: Jossey-Bass, 2012), 53.

9. Robert Schnase, *Five Practices of Fruitful Congregations* (Nashville, TN: Abingdon Press, 2007), 8.

10. Gil Rendle and Alice Mann, *Holy Conversations: Strategic Planning as a Spiritual Practice for Congregations* (Bethesda, MD: Alban Institute, 2003). See also chapter 5 of this book for further discussion.

11. C. Kirk Hadaway, *Facts on Growth: 2010* (Hartford, CT: Hartford Institute for Religion Research, 2011), 8.

CHAPTER 3

1. Jeffrey Bullock, "How We Make Choices: Congregations and the Psychology of Risk," *Christian Century* 130, no. 12 (June 12, 2013): 12–13.

2. Report of the Team Vital to the Council of Bishops, May 2013.

3. Leonora Tubbs Tisdale, *Preaching as Local Theology and Folk Art* (Minneapolis, MN: Fortress Press, 1997), xii.

4. Barry Schwartz and Kenneth Sharpe, *Practical Wisdom: The Right Way to Do the Right Thing* (New York: Riverhead Books, 2010), 4.

5. Ibid., 5.

6. Ibid.

7. Ibid., 7.

8. William Duggan, *Strategic Intuition: The Creative Spark in Human Achievement* (New York: Columbia Business School Publishing, 2007), 2.

9. Ibid., 106.

10. Charles Murray, *Coming Apart: The State of White America, 1960–2010* (New York: Crown Forum, 2012).

11. Steve Rothschild, *The Non Nonprofit: For-Profit Thinking for Nonprofit Success* (San Francisco: Jossey-Bass, 2012), 23.

12. Gil Rendle and Susan Beaumont, *When Moses Meets Aaron: Staffing and Supervision in Large Congregations* (Herndon, VA: Alban Institute, 2007), 101–2.

CHAPTER 4

1. David Brooks, "What Data Can't Do," *New York Times*, February 18, 2013.

2. Thomas Davenport and Laurence Prusak, *Working Knowledge: How Organizations Manage What They Know* (Boston: Harvard Business School Press, 1998), 2–6.

3. Ibid., 4.

4. Lovett Weems, "The Tussle over Metrics," *Lewis Center Update*, May 2, 2012.

5. Maxwell Anderson, *Metrics of Success in Art Museums* (Los Angeles: Getty Leadership Institute, 2004).

6. Ibid., 2.

7. Ibid., 9.

8. Bishop Michael Lowry, "Assessing Conference Faithfulness and Fruitfulness," (working document).

9. Jim Collins, "Good to Great and the Social Sectors," www.jimcollins.com, 2005.

10. John Guaspari, *I Know It When I See It: A Modern Fable about Quality* (New York: AMACOM, 1985).

11. Atul Gawande, *Better: A Surgeon's Notes on Performance* (New York: Henry Holt, 2007), 190.

12. Gil Rendle and Alice Mann, *Holy Conversations: Strategic Planning as a Spiritual Practice for Congregations* (Bethesda, MD: Alban Institute, 2003), 211–16.

13. C. Kirk Hadaway, *Facts on Growth: 2010* (Hartford, CT: Hartford Institute for Religion Research, 2011).

14. Robert Penna and William Phillips, *Outcome Frameworks: An Overview for Practitioners* (Delmar, NY: Rensselaerville Institute, 2004), 35.

15. Wade Clark Roof, "Religion and Narrative," *Review of Religious Research* 34, no. 4 (June 1993): 3.

16. Penna and Phillips, *Outcome Frameworks*, 74.

17. Peter Drucker, *Managing the Non-Profit Organization: Principles and Practices* (New York: Harper Business, 1990), xiv.

CHAPTER 5

1. Michael Fullan, *Leading in a Culture of Change* (San Francisco: Jossey-Bass, 2001), 52.

2. Patrick Lencioni, *The Advantage: Why Organizational Health Trumps Everything Else in Business* (San Francisco: Jossey-Bass, 2012).

3. Ibid., 78.

4. Gil Rendle and Alice Mann, *Holy Conversations: Strategic Planning as a Spiritual Practice for Congregations* (Bethesda, MD: Alban Institute, 2003).

CHAPTER 6

1. Martin Luther King, Jr., "A Knock at Midnight," in *Strength to Love* (Minneapolis, MN: Fortress Press, 2010), 56.
2. Mary Walton, *The Deming Management Method* (New York: Perigee Books, 1986).
3. W. Edwards Deming, *Out of Crisis* (Cambridge, MA: Massachusetts Institute of Technology Center for Advanced Engineering Study, 1982), 97–99.
4. Ibid., 99.
5. Ibid., 121.
6. Ibid., 105.
7. Daniel Pink, *Drive: The Surprising Truth about What Motivates Us* (New York: Riverhead Books, 2009), 2.
8. Ibid., 27.
9. Ibid., 48.
10. Barry Schwartz and Kenneth Sharpe, *Practical Wisdom: The Right Way to Do the Right Thing* (New York: Riverhead Books, 2010), 28.
11. King, "A Knock at Midnight," 61.

Bibliography

Anderson, Maxwell. *Metrics of Success in Art Museums*. Los Angeles: Getty Leadership Institute, 2004.

Beeley, Christopher. *Leading God's People: Wisdom from the Early Church for Today*. Grand Rapids, MI: Eerdman's, 2012.

Brooks, David. "What Data Can't Do," *New York Times*, February 18, 2013.

Bullock, Jeffrey. "How We Make Choices: Congregations and the Psychology of Risk," *Christian Century* 130, no. 12 (June 12, 2013).

Coffin, William Sloane. *Credo*. Louisville, KY: Westminster John Knox Press, 2004.

Collins, Jim. "Good to Great and the Social Sectors." www.jimcollins.com, 2005.

Davenport, Thomas and Laurence Prusak. *Working Knowledge: How Organizations Manage What They Know*. Boston: Harvard Business School Press, 1998.

Deming, W. Edwards. *Out of Crisis*. Cambridge, MA: Massachusetts Institute of Technology Center for Advanced Engineering Study, 1982.

Drucker, Peter. *Managing the Non-Profit Organization: Principles and Practices*. New York: Harper Business, 1990.

Duggan, William. *Strategic Intuition: The Creative Spark in Human Achievement*. New York: Columbia Business School Publishing, 2007.

Fullan, Michael. *Leading in a Culture of Change*. San Francisco: Jossey-Bass, 2001.

Garenta, Beverly Roberts and David Peterson, eds. *The New Interpreter's Bible One-Volume Commentary*. Nashville, TN: Abingdon Press, 2010.

Gawande, Atul. *Better: A Surgeon's Notes on Performance*. New York: Henry Holt, 2007.

Guaspari, John. *I Know It When I See It: A Modern Fable about Quality*. New York: AMACOM, 1985.

Hadaway, C. Kirk. *Facts on Growth: 2010*. Hartford, CT: Hartford Institute for Religion Research, 2011.

King, Martin Luther, Jr. *Strength to Love*. Minneapolis, MN: Fortress Press, 2010.

Lencioni, Patrick. *The Advantage: Why Organizational Health Trumps Everything Else in Business*. San Francisco: Jossey-Bass, 2012.

McNeil, Reggie. *Missional Renaissance: Changing the Scorecard for the Church*. San Francisco: Jossey-Bass, 2009.

Murray, Charles. *Coming Apart: The State of White America, 1960–2010*. New York: Crown Forum, 2012.

Penna, Robert and William Phillips. *Outcome Frameworks: An Overview for Practitioners*. Delmar, New York: Rensselaerville Institute, 2004.

Pink, Daniel. *Drive: The Surprising Truth about What Motivates Us*. New York: Riverhead Books, 2009.

Rendle, Gil. *Back to Zero: The Search to Rediscover the Methodist Movement*. Nashville, TN: Abingdon Press, 2011.

Rendle, Gil and Susan Beaumont. *When Moses Meets Aaron: Staffing and Supervision in Large Congregations*. Herndon, VA: Alban Institute, 2007.

Rendle, Gil and Alice Mann. *Holy Conversations: Strategic Planning as a Spiritual Practice for Congregations*. Bethesda, MD: Alban Institute, 2003.

Roof, Wade Clark. "Religion and Narrative," *Review of Religious Research* 34, no. 4 (June 1993).

Rothschild, Steve. *The Non Nonprofit: For-Profit Thinking for Nonprofit Success*. San Francisco: Jossey-Bass, 2012.

Schnase, Robert. *Five Practices of Fruitful Congregations*. Nashville, TN: Abingdon Press, 2007.

Schwartz, Barry and Kenneth Sharpe. *Practical Wisdom: The Right Way to Do the Right Thing*. New York: Riverhead Books, 2010.

Szanto, Andras. "Art Basel," *Miami Beach Daily*, December 1, 2011.

Tisdale, Leonora Tubbs. *Preaching as Local Theology and Folk Art*. Minneapolis, MN: Fortress Press, 1997.

Walton, Mary. *The Deming Management Method*. New York: Perigee Books, 1986.

Weems, Lovett. "The Tussle over Metrics," *Lewis Center Update*, May 2, 2012.

About the Author

Gil Rendle serves as senior consultant with the Texas Methodist Foundation in Austin, Texas, and as an independent consultant working with denominational leaders on issues of change and leadership. Prior to this position, he served the Alban Institute as an author, seminar leader and senior consultant for twelve years. An ordained United Methodist minister, Rendle served as senior pastor of two urban congregations in Pennsylvania and as a denominational consultant for the United Methodist Church.

Rendle has an extensive background in organizational development, group-and-systems theory and leadership development. He has consulted with congregations on planning, staff-and-leadership development and issues of change. He is well known for his work with middle judicatory and national denominational offices and staff as they wrestle with denominational and congregational change. He is the author of seven books, a contributor to four books and the author of numerous articles and monographs. His most recent books include *Journey in the Wilderness: New Life for Mainline Churches* (2010) and *Back to Zero: The Search to Rediscover the Methodist Movement* (2011). Gil is a resident of Pennsylvania, where he lives with his wife, Lynne.